Narcissist Recovery

How to Stop the Aggressive Narcissist, Finding the Energy to Heal after Any Covert Emotional and Psychological Abuse. Take Back Your Life from Passive Codependency!

DEBBIE BRAIN

Table of Contents

Introduction

Has your partner ever left you feeling ashamed, fearful, or worthless? Has your partner ever made you feel as though you can never do anything right? No matter how hard you may try, you constantly are met with criticism and being told that you could have done better had you tried a little more. You give your all, and yet you are constantly demeaned and criticized to the point that you feel as though you may as well give up and just accept your own insufficiencies. You are taught that your own feelings do not matter and that ultimately, the other person is the only one allowed to make decisions, and you must go along with them no matter what. Even at restaurants, you may find that your partner orders your food for you with no input from you. Does this sound familiar? If it does, you may have a narcissistic abuser in your life.

Narcissistic abusers do not care about their victims. They want what they want, and they expect everyone else to cater to those wants. They do not hesitate to lie, cheat on their partners, steal, manipulate, threaten, blackmail, or even physically hurt other people in order to get what they want. Even those closest to the narcissist, romantic partners, children, and friends, are not exempt from the abuse. If anything, they are more likely to catch the abuser's eye and be on the receiving end of any manipulation.

If you believe that you have a narcissist in your life and you are ready to heal, this is the book for you. Within this book, you will be guided through identifying narcissists and their abusive behaviors. You will learn the ins and outs of handling abuse as it happens, as well as how to avoid abuse altogether. More importantly, you will learn how to recover.

Recovering from narcissistic abuse is a long, arduous road, but it is worthwhile. Through healing, you will rediscover your passion for living and your own inherent value. You will learn how to respect and take care of yourself in order to begin your journey toward healing. Remember, you do not deserve to be abused, nor do you have to put up with the narcissist's manipulation attempts. You are well within your rights to decide that enough is enough and make an effort to protect yourself.

Life does not require the narcissist to continue. You can live without him or her, despite what the narcissist may have convinced you. You are enough. You are worthy of respect and to be treated with basic human decency.

If you have decided that you have finally had enough of the narcissist's abuse, you are ready to move on with the steps that will be addressed in this book. Good luck on this journey, and remember to have patience and compassion for yourself. This is a long process, and you will not see results overnight. Do not lose faith, though— the results will happen if you stay resolute and put in the work.

Part I

The Narcissist's Abuse

Chapter 1: Narcissistic Personality Disorder

Narcissists are individuals who suffer from narcissistic personality disorder. They typically have behaviors that meet three distinct traits. They lack empathy, or their ability to feel empathy is compromised and limited in some fashion. They crave attention, seeking it out from anyone and everyone around them and needing it to validate their own existence. They are grandiose, meaning that they feel as though they are better, more special, more unique, and overall superior to those around them.

The narcissist, particularly when he wants to get something that has been met with resistance, tends to manipulate others. He sees the world, and his own position within the world, through a distorted lens and does not function in a normal capacity. There is no treating a narcissist, particularly when he is too stubborn or unable to see his own fault due to believing that he is perfect. His perceived perfectionism is used to justify that he does not have a problem, and if confronted and told that he needs therapy, which would be the only real way he could make real, noticeable changes, he would deny it and point all of his delusions of perfection and grandeur as justification for them.

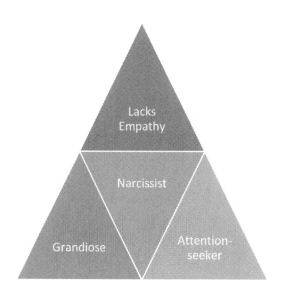

Who is the Narcissist?

The narcissist as an individual is somewhat difficult for many people to understand, but at his heart, he has three key tenets to his personality. He is reactive when criticized, he lacks self-esteem, and he responds to challenging his perception of reality with rage and abuse. The narcissist, despite his typical façade of being better than everyone else, is actually quite sensitive. Because of his sensitivity, he has a tendency to react strongly when things do not go his way. When you want to understand the narcissist, you want to consider these three traits.

Reactive to criticism

Narcissists do not want to feel criticized. They believe they are superior for one reason or another, and any time they are criticized, whether constructively or otherwise, they take it as a personal affront to themselves. Even the most well-intentioned constructive criticism, such as providing advice as to whether the narcissist should try a new method at work that is more efficient is somehow twisted in order to make the narcissist feel as though he has been wronged or victimized. Rather than seeing it as an attempt to help or better the narcissist, he instead sees it as an attack and responds accordingly.

When criticized, the narcissist is going to turn things somehow around, so the other person is actually the attacker. The narcissist believes that even being corrected or criticized is the same thing as attacking the other person and sees it as incredibly disrespectful.

Lacks self-esteem

A lot of the reason the narcissist struggles with criticism is that his self-esteem is lacking or is fragile and easily harmed. Even though he wholeheartedly believes that he is superior, it is easy to damage that belief because of his weak self-esteem. Even the slightest perceived criticism hurts the narcissist at his core. Think of self-esteem as a shield between your innermost, sensitive core, and the external world. When your self-esteem is weak, it is easy for criticism to hurt your feelings. You take it personally, and you feel hurt just for being criticized at all. Instead of being able to rely on your self-esteem to shield you somewhat so you can see the criticism through a clear mind, you instead find yourself vulnerable when that self-esteem is deficient or lacking.

This is exactly what happens with the narcissist. He seeks to protect himself through his behaviors and beliefs of grandeur; they are sorts of coping mechanisms for that lack of self-esteem. While they do bolster up his confidence for a while, he must then go out and seek validation from other people, craving admiration to make him feel as though he is worthwhile. The self-esteem usually tells you that you are sufficient, and reminds you that you do deserve to be treated with a certain standard of decency, and when your self-esteem is fragile or broken, you do not have that to rely on. You instead need to seek validation from other people instead, who tell you that you are valuable or worthwhile to them, and that is enough to make you feel better, at least for a little while until the next wave of low self-esteem hits.

This is exactly how the narcissist sneaks through life. While he is outwardly abusive to other people, particularly when manipulating them, he is doing it to compensate for his fractured self-esteem. That lack of healthy self-esteem means that he cannot see value in himself without being valued by others. His lack of empathy means he does not care if he hurts other people. He just wants to feel as though he is wanted and valued to feel better about himself. This, of course, does not excuse his behavior, but it does provide a way to understand the mindset behind the behaviors.

Responds with rage

When the narcissist does not get the desired result, he wants or is challenged in some way, shape, or form, his default reaction is rage. He will abuse other people, lash out, physically or emotionally hurt others, or do anything else he thinks is necessary to force reality into his own paradigm.

Remember, narcissists, do not see reality the way it actually is. Everything around them is distorted into ways that make sense to the narcissist and justify his behaviors. He would rather manipulate himself into believing his lies than actually facing reality, and so he does. He wants to manipulate others into seeing the world his way, as that allows for him to continue living in his delusional world. Anything that denies his delusions is faced with the same ferocity as someone who has just been told that any of their other core beliefs are false. Imagine someone who just learned that his child is not actually his child—he likely responds in anger. So too does the narcissist respond to any sort of challenge to his own delusional beliefs.

Diagnosing the Narcissist

As a certified personality disorder, there are diagnostic criteria for the narcissist. Diagnosing the narcissist involves looking at a series of traits and attempting to identify them in the assumed narcissist. In order to be diagnosed, the person must exhibit at least five of the nine symptoms or traits listed, and those traits must be pervasive. Being pervasive means, they persist, regardless of context. They are repeated, and occur in several different contexts, meaning that they are inherent parts of the individual's personality instead of being seen as a product of the environment. The nine traits of NPD include the following: Delusions of grandeur, obsessions with fantasies, a belief of uniqueness, a need for attention, entitlement, exploitative or manipulative, lacking empathy, being envious of others while projecting his own envy on other people, and arrogance or haughtiness.

Delusions of grandeur

Delusions of grandeur involve beliefs that the narcissist is better than everyone else. The narcissist sees himself as the best person in the world and constantly has to be better than those around him. He refuses to acknowledge when someone else beats him or is better than him, as he is too perfect to be beaten through legitimate means. If someone has won, they must have cheated. The narcissist also uses these delusions to justify that he can never be at fault, as perfection is never wrong.

Obsession with Fantasies

Just as the narcissist believes that he is perfect and superior, he believes that he should have everything he fantasizes over. He dreams of absolute power, love, money, perfection, and superiority, and constantly strives to achieve them, though not very hard. He believes that he is inherently deserving of those things and instead expects them to come to him. He is frequently disappointed when these fantasies never come to fruition because he is expecting things that are nearly unattainable for the average person.

Believes he is unique

The narcissist believes that he is unique in all situations. He is able to justify this by his beliefs of superiority, and he uses those beliefs of being unique as a way to discredit others. If someone disagrees with him, he sees it as someone not understanding his ingenuity. If someone calls him out on something, it is because they do not know better. It even extends to victimizing himself— when something bad happens, he has it worse than everyone else, and he will prove it in an argument, lamenting everything that ever happened in his life, even if the challenges he laments are relatively normal or expected.

Requires attention

The narcissist craves attention from all around him. Remember, this is what he uses to soothe his fragile ego, especially when he feels as though his ego has been slighted or harmed in any way. He will do whatever it takes to always be the center of attention, even if it involves pretending to faint or creating a dramatic situation.

Entitled

Though the narcissist wants it all, he does not want to put in the effort. He believes he should get anything his heart desires just because he is him. He expects to be handed whatever he desires on a golden platter. If he applies for a job, he expects to get it, even if he is not qualified. He believes he can get whatever woman (or man) he wants simply because he is deserving of the perfect partner. He sees those around him as tools to get what he believes is owed to him, and he wants to do it with the least amount of effort possible.

Exploitative and Manipulative

When he is not simply given what he feels like he deserves, the narcissist resorts to manipulation to get his way. He will lie, guilt, intimidate, threaten, and exploit other people if that is all that stands between himself and whatever it is, he is trying to obtain, be it narcissistic supply, a job, or even a partner. The narcissist wants it all, after all, and he will attempt to get it.

Lacks Empathy

The narcissist cannot empathize with other people. He may understand on a fundamental level how his actions make others feel, as he has to in order to effectively manipulate them, but he does not relate. He does not feel the pangs of sorrow when he sees a picture of a grieving spouse, or feel the joy when watching a child finally succeed at something he has been attempting for hours. The narcissist only knows his own feelings, and even then, he struggles with them frequently.

Envious of others, and often projects his own envy onto other people

The narcissist often looks at other people who have what he wants and feels envious. However, he usually manages to manipulate that envy around in order to soothe his own ego. He tells himself that the other person must be envious of him instead, and will gaslight himself into believing it. For example, if he applies to a new job that he really wants and gets passed over, he reminds himself that at least his current job does not come with long weekends, evening, and require travel like the one he had applied for, and that the other person is going to be jealous of his lack of responsibility as soon as the workload increases.

Arrogant

Due to believing that he is infallible and superior to all, he often comes across as arrogant or haughty. He does not see the point in respecting his inferiors and does not waste the mental energy in doing so. If the other people wanted to be deserving of respect, he tells himself, they would have worked harder to be worthy of it.

Identifying the Narcissist

When trying to identify a narcissist, the most effective method is to look for the traits listed previously, as well as using the WEB method. The WEB method involves words, emotions, and behaviors. You first identify their words, then your emotions, and their behaviors.

Words
- Look at the kind of words they are using
- Positive, negative, uninterested, etc.

Emotions
- Look at your emotions in response to their words
- Feeling happy, anxious, guilty

Behaviors
- Look at how they react
- Frustrated often, blaming others, demanding

Focus on their words

When you want to see if someone in your midst is a narcissist, look at their words. You should see how the person is speaking. The narcissist frequently works in extremes with a little grey area. They are either incredibly positive or absolutely demeaning. They want to raise you up and make you feel almost high on the attention, or they want to tear you down so thoroughly, you do not know what hit them. Narcissists struggle with mood regulation, and this shows in their words.

- **Extremely positive:** The narcissist will talk about things in terms of grandiosity. They raise up themselves or you during this kind of speak. They may sing your praises or sing their own to make them look more desirable. These words are meant to hook you to them.

- **Extremely negative:** These are the words used to keep you in line. They use these to ruin the other person's sense of self. These may be directed toward you or toward other people. If you hear someone speaking incredibly negatively about someone else, you should be wary, as you will likely be on the receiving end at some point.

- **Uninterested:** The narcissist may constantly change the subject or show a lack of empathy. The narcissist may shrug off what is being said and instead change the subject back to themselves. This disregards any concerns that are brought to them if there are any.

- **Victimizing:** These are words used to convince the narcissist that he is the victim in the situation. He may tell himself that the world unfairly caused his failure, and he will believe it. He may also use these words to flip around an argument with someone to change from the aggressor to the victim.

Watch your emotions

While paying close attention to the narcissist's choice in words, pay attention to how your own mood fluctuates around him. If you think the narcissist seems unreal, larger than life, or too good to be true, there is likely a good reason for it. Trust your gut. If you are going through extreme mood swings, going from feeling like the most loved person in the world down to feeling worse than dirt, then there is probably a reason for this as well. While your mood will always somewhat be influenced by a romantic partner, most partners do not intentionally try to manipulate feelings or have them oscillate so drastically. If you feel yourself growing anxious around the person you suspect is a narcissist, that is a pretty good sign that there is something wrong in the situation, and you should trust your instinct.

Watch their behaviors

Lastly, pay attention to how the narcissist acts. Oftentimes, the narcissist will say one thing while doing the opposite. For example, he may be exclaiming how much he loves you while glaring at you or holding himself in an aggressive manner. His words will not always line up with his behaviors, and he often uses a barrage of words in order to distract the other person from what he is doing.

In particular, you should look for behaviors that show that the narcissist is dangerous. Is he explosive? Easily frustrated? Can he handle a change? If he is showing behaviors that point toward narcissistic tendencies, such as manipulating, disregarding other people, or blaming other people while victimizing himself, you have a pretty good indicator that he is a narcissist.

Chapter 2: Types of Narcissists

Narcissism is a spectrum—there are several different ways a narcissist could present to others. Some of them prefer to manipulate others openly, not particularly caring what other people think or feel, so long as they are the center of attention. Others feel an intense need to be valued by others and are a lot more covert in their attempts to get what they want. Others still simply want to wreak havoc any way they can with no regard for consequences or authority.

All types of narcissists share the same diagnostic criteria—if they are a diagnosed narcissist, they have at least five of the nine traits listed in the previous chapter, and they are, to some degree, similar. What matters is how each type of narcissist decides to present those symptoms. The three types of narcissists are the exhibitionist narcissist, the closet narcissist, and the toxic narcissist.

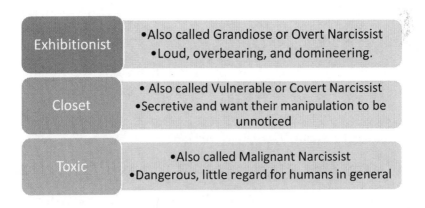

Exhibitionist	• Also called Grandiose or Overt Narcissist • Loud, overbearing, and domineering.
Closet	• Also called Vulnerable or Covert Narcissist • Secretive and want their manipulation to be unnoticed
Toxic	• Also called Malignant Narcissist • Dangerous, little regard for humans in general

Exhibitionist Narcissist

The exhibitionist narcissist wants attention at all times. He demands attention and admiration and expects to get it. Since he is clearly superior to everyone else, as justified by his delusions of grandeur, he expects everyone to give him what he wants. He sees himself as deserving of being showered in attention and has convinced even himself that he is better than everyone else. What may once have started out as a tool or way to convince others that he is worthy has morphed into someone who believes that he is the best in every way. The exhibition narcissist is loud about his achievements. He boasts of all the reasons he deserves to be lavished with praises and expects them in return. He frequently seeks out jobs in fields that command attention or respect, such as executives, doctors, lawyers, or other high-profile jobs, and he uses that position to leverage himself into the deserving more narcissistic supply to feed his fragile ego.

His ego only feels soothed when he is being praised or very briefly afterward. He needs to feel as though he is admired as if people around him all see that he is such a good person, and he will manipulate them into doing so. He wants this admiration so much that he would rather have it under false pretenses than not at all. This is why he is so willing to manipulate others. Since he personally has no problems with manipulating others since he does not feel empathy that cues him to stop or feel guilty, he is willing to do it to get what he wants. He sees people as a means to an end and uses them as such.

Ultimately, the exhibitionist narcissist does not care that people actually like him, so long as they respect him and his inherent authority. He believes that authority has been graced to him and that he deserves every moment of the spotlight he can get, and then some. He will not try to hide his desire for control from others, instead of seeing it as authority that should command respect and admiration. Unfortunately, especially when the narcissist does land a position in which he has authority, this use comes across as dictatorship rather than anything remotely resembling good leadership because he struggles to empathize. He sees everyone he has power over as little more than tools, particularly if he is in the workplace. If he has legitimized authority, such as being a supervisor, he expects his employees to ask, "How high?" any time he asks them to jump.

Oftentimes, the exhibitionist narcissist has grown up being told that he is superior, and after hearing it enough, he began to believe it. After being given it, especially at a young age, he may have developed a narcissistic personality in return. His own superiority was likely encouraged earlier in life, whether he was good at school or sports, and he used that as justification that he was superior in all ways. He also will expect that one success, or one instance of superiority, is enough to justify his superiority indefinitely. If he got a touchdown once in high school that won a game, he is likely to insist that he is still superior, even ten years later because of that one instance.

The exhibitionist narcissist, in particular, has managed to convince himself that his distortions are real. He sees that he is superior and convinces himself of such. Even if things go wrong or not as expected, the exhibitionist narcissist, in particular, will make it a point to convince himself that the result is actually the one he wanted all along. He sees the misalignment between his expectations and reality, and in this instance, actually manages to alter his expectations to align. This saves him from the typical explosion when met with confrontation, and he is able to move on.

For example, if the narcissist had an expectation of buying a new house and has gotten into a bidding war that he eventually loses, rather than explode, he looks at the fact that he has lost and declares that he did not really want the house anyway and the ones on the market are far nice, even if this is not the case. He will legitimately gaslight himself into believing something if he has to in order to make everyone else think he still maintains his expectation of perfection. In the end, he is able to say that things went exactly according to plan, though most people likely will not believe him. In his mind, this fixes the disconnect between what happened and his expectations, though everyone around him probably spent a few minutes wondering why he would bid on a house he did not actually want.

The exhibitionist narcissist, in particular, also engages in what is known as magical thinking. This sort of thinking describes the thought process of wishing for something and therefore expecting it to happen. Just as a child may think that she can wish on a star for a pony and fully expects to wake up to one in the morning, the narcissist has developed an expectation that if he thinks about it, he will get it. This is his entitlement in action—If he wants the job, he will get the job, and if he does not get the job, it is because he really did not want it anyway.

Closet Narcissist

The closet narcissist, on the other hand, is far more sensitive than the exhibitionist narcissist. The closet narcissist is so concerned with being rejected by others, or feeling as though he is at risk of being abandoned at any moment that he is constantly swinging back and forth between feeling as though he is superior to his peers or inferior. His own self-worth is constantly swinging like a pendulum with the ebb and flow of attention and validation sought after by other people. When the narcissist feels inferior, he feels the need to validate himself through other people's attention. After being validated, he gets to ride a short period of feeling superior once again.

When the closet narcissist seeks the attention of someone else, the preferred tactic to earn it is through playing the victim. The closet narcissist prefers for manipulation to be more covert and emotional, being undetected by the ones being manipulated until it is too late, and the easiest way to do this is by playing the victim and appealing to other people's sense of pitying him. When he is pitied, after all, people that value him come to his rescue to help. He sees the act of someone fixing his problem or saving him as validating him as a worthwhile person in the eyes of others, which he then uses to keep himself feeling superior.

Ultimately, the closet narcissist is a person with an ego that has been so broken that he feels the need to pretend he is someone else in order to be valued. Narcissists of all kinds engage in mirroring, and the closet narcissist is no exception. Feeling so vulnerable, the closet narcissist thinks that the only way anyone would ever willingly come to his aid is if he played the victim. This persona that the narcissist builds up is meant to be the perfect victim—someone who is always a result of bad circumstances and luck who is never truly at fault for anything.

Unlike the exhibitionist narcissist, however, the closet narcissist does legitimately worry about how other people see him. He is self-conscious and afraid that people will discover his true self and reject him, and because of that, he fights tooth and nail to protect his persona's integrity at all costs. He will build rapport with other people, seeking to create good relationships with others, and develop a surrounding of people that will back him up if he needs to. He wants to make sure that others see him favorably in order to maintain his persona. The closet narcissist will make it a point to encourage and develop relationships, and while the relationships may not be as meaningful as a non-narcissist's, they do attempt it.

Also contrasting from the exhibitionist narcissist, the closet narcissist cannot stand the idea of change. If anything goes wrong or does not work out according to plans, the closet narcissist is likely to react violently. He cannot cope with the idea of failing or not getting his way, and the more things slip out of his control, the more desperately he will attempt to force things back to fit his expectations. He will start covertly, starting with guilt trips or gaslighting, and slowly escalate to passive-aggressive comments, and eventually escalating to smear campaigns and even possibly escalating to physical abuse if necessary. What the closet narcissist wants is conformity, and if he does not get that, he does not understand how to cope with the truth. He cannot imagine a situation in which he is wrong, nor can he comprehend a way to manage the situation in any way except violently.

This is when the closet narcissist becomes dangerous, as when he does not get his way, all bets and pretenses are off. He will lose his mask or be unable to maintain it, and all that is left is an individual who feels so incredibly wronged and slighted that he will do anything to retaliate and fix things to get what he wants.

Ultimately, the goal of the closet narcissist is to be great. They want to be seen as a valuable member of society, so people are convinced to do their bidding willingly rather than having to be forced into it. They want to be loved, wanted, and valued for them, but they feel as though they never can be due to their self-esteem. Instead, they set up their persona to be likable while they sit back and walk through life, living a pretense.

Toxic Narcissist

The last type of narcissist that will be discussed here is the toxic narcissist. While the previous two narcissists are sometimes annoying and exhausting, as well as difficult to deal with, the toxic narcissist is destructive. Toxic narcissists thrive on watching other people suffer. They are vicious and have no regard for human life. They do not care if people feel disrespected or unwanted; in fact, they thrive on it. They want other people to feel devalued and hurt so they can sit back and laugh.

The toxic narcissist genuinely enjoys hurting other people. Torment and suffering bring a smile to the toxic narcissist's face, and he would love to watch the world burn if he could arrange to happen without hurting himself. The toxic narcissist will typically present himself as normal, charismatic, and likable, much like the other narcissists, but he uses this in order to get in close enough to hurt other people. Much like the exhibitionist narcissist, the toxic narcissist wants authority. He wants to be seen as in charge, respected and appreciated. He wants attention in general, but he will also accept negative attention as an acceptable alternative if positive is not possible. He will make it a point to present himself as successful, striving for high-power roles, but this does nothing to assuage his deeply fractured self-esteem.

Like the closet narcissist, the toxic narcissist feels fragile, and he does not cope well with change. He struggles if things do not go his way, and if he feels he is losing control, he is far happier outwardly sabotaging the entire situation than allowing control to slip away. He would rather destroy the thing he is losing than allow it to leave. For example, in a divorce, he may decide to ruin his ex-spouse, lying to everyone who will listen, attempting to take the children away, trying to manipulate the children that he likely does not even want into living with him, and may even literally destroy property just to prove the point. If they have to split something, he would rather take literally half of every single thing and leave it all unusable for everyone than take half of the things. For example, imagine the couple is splitting Lego sets—The toxic narcissist would far prefer just to take literally half of the blocks in each set rather than being the rational person and taking half of the complete sets. He does not mind if he suffers too so long as the person who has escaped his control is also miserable, and he has left her suffering as well.

In reality, this desire for other people to hurt is an inherent flaw with his personality. He only feels better when he is able to exert control over a situation, and hurting other people is a form of validation of power for him. In the eyes of the toxic narcissist, being in a position of being able to inflict harm onto someone else so intimately as he seeks to do to his relationship partners is a true sign of power—He can literally control whether the other person feels safe and the other person's wellbeing. This is the ultimate form of power to the narcissist, and he is happy to exert it at any chance he gets.

The toxic narcissist has a blatant disregard for any sort of social conventions. Ultimately, social conventions are seen as boundaries, and the toxic narcissist prefers to nuke those boundaries into oblivion. He will steal, lie, cheat, and hurt other people before he allows someone else to dictate what he does, and sometimes he will do all of those things just because he can. Toxic narcissists have the potential to become serial killers, rapists, or form terrorist organizations just because they can, with little motivation other than being able to do so. They feel gratification in hurting other people, and that sadistic pleasure is what encourages them to act in ways that blatantly violate social conventions.

The toxic narcissist, unlike the other narcissists who seek to manipulate to serve a purpose, will manipulate others just because he can. He sees it as a game and will proactively seek out opportunities to manipulate others just to see if he can. If he is met with resistance when he does try to manipulate another person, he is likely to push back harder and harder until he literally beats the person into submission if he feels the need or desire to do so.

This narcissist should be avoided at all costs. The toxic narcissist loves to watch people hurt and has no qualms at harming others himself and is capable of killing a person for sport. With no regard to standard social conventions, he is willing to do anything to get what he wants and is willing to cater to any impulse he may feel going about his day.

Chapter 3: Narcissistic Abuse

Narcissists have endless ways they abuse others. They use abuse to get people in line and ensure that they get their way. Though the toxic narcissist, in particular, prefers to abuse people for sport, most of the times, narcissistic abuse is opportunistic. The narcissist is using it as a tool or a weapon against his victim. He does not care what the result is, but he is not necessarily doing it to be mean-spirited intentionally or just to hurt someone; the harm is collateral damage in manipulating the other person into doing what he wants. His end goal is typically getting whatever he desires, not hurting people. Most narcissists are far too interested in their own feelings to worry about hurting other people's just to hurt them, and narcissists are typically much more preoccupied with themselves anyway. Nevertheless, all of these manipulation techniques have the potential to inflict serious physical or emotional harm if used against other people. This list is by no means comprehensive, but these are some of the most commonly used abuse tactics.

Verbal Abuse

The intention of verbal abuse is to break down the target into submission. It is frequently used to make the other person feel insecure enough that they give in simply because they do not feel as though they are worthy of anything else. Verbal abuse has many different forms that it can take, and all of them are particularly harmful and serves to make the victim wonder if they are to blame, or if they are overreacting in general.

Verbal abuse almost always takes place in private since no one else is around to hear or witness it, allowing for the narcissist to deny its existence if necessary. This also creates an isolation effect with the victim, as the victim feels as though he or she cannot reach out to others because there is no proof of what was said. Verbal abuse may not often happen at first, but it eventually escalates to the point that it is a typical method of communication, particularly when in private.

The victims of verbal abuse frequently rationalize the abuse as being an acceptable form of communication, but it is still difficult for the victims to deal with at the moment. They may not recognize that it is essentially another form of exerting control over the situation and over the victim.

There are several different types of verbal abuse, some of which are easier than others to identify. Here are several abuse patterns as well as an example of what they may look like at the moment:

- Name-calling: "Wow, you're such an idiot! You never learn, do you?"

- Manipulation: "If you loved me, you would do this for me, even if you don't want to."

- Demeaning comments: "Wow, you're such a typical girl—you can't even remember to get your oil changed in your car. No wonder it broke down again."

- Condescending: "Hah, no wonder you always complain about struggling with your schoolwork— you can't even figure out how to double a recipe!"

- Unconstructive, cruel criticism: "Can't you do anything right? You're always able to bring down the mood with one stupid mistake, aren't you?"

- Threats: "You won't like what happens if you do that." Or "I will kill myself if you ever try to leave."

- Blame: "It's your fault we never have any money for anything fun." Or "Look at what you made me do! I would never have done it if you had just listened."

- Silent treatment: Your partner intentionally avoids talking to you to make you miserable.

Covert Aggression

Covert aggression involves behaviors that are meant to be aggressive but are less noticeable that hitting or directly harming or threatening someone. In covert aggression, the abuser seeks to conceal the abuse, and because it is meant to be secretive, it frequently involves various layers of manipulation. Covert aggression can be difficult to identify when you are being victimized, especially if the narcissist constantly denies any abuse is happening. However, there are several ways you can identify covert aggression in the act, or in which covert aggression can manifest. If you can identify these, you will understand how to see covert aggression as it occurs.

Lies to you

The most obvious form of covert aggression is in lying. When the narcissist lies, he falsifies the way something has happened. He changes the truth and denies what the victim believes to have happened. It allows for hiding of the truth as well, which can never be healthy or beneficial. Even minor lies, such as about which grocery store you went to, can build up and degrade trust over time. Ultimately, relationships are built upon trust, and lies threaten that foundation. Lying also usually results in conflict at some point. When the truth comes out, there is almost always some form of conflict as a result.

Blames you

By pushing the blame onto the victim, the narcissist is able to escape fault. This is the way that the narcissist can evade taking responsibility for his actions, even though it eventually lands on the victim and inflicts harm. By becoming the victim instead of taking responsibility, the narcissist is able to look better in that particular situation and may even be able to get some sympathy or narcissistic supply from other people.

If you are constantly being blamed for situations when you are certain they were not your fault, you may be the victim of covert aggression.

Embarrasses you

The abuser will sometimes seek to embarrass you. The reason for this is it dehumanizes you—it allows the narcissist to feel as though he is superior to you, which grants him perceived power and also serves to injure your self-esteem. This is the narcissist seeking to take advantage of anything you have done, whether it is a mistake or even some perceived, made up weakness the narcissist has suddenly decided you have.

In embarrassing you, such as in making fun of you when out with other people, the narcissist seeks to humiliate and belittle you, while still being able to pretend it was a joke if you try to argue in any way or stand up for yourself. While he pretends, it was a joke; there was actually much more than that behind the surface.

Seduces you

This type of covert aggression involves flattering you just to get what the narcissist wants. He may tell you that you look beautiful five minutes before demanding you do something tedious for him. The flattering or seduction is not genuine and is strictly used to warm you up, so you are more willing to do whatever the narcissist wants.

While this may not seem outwardly or even inwardly aggressive, the aggressive nature of this lies in the fact that the narcissist is toying with your emotions, using them to get whatever it is that he wants from you. He is essentially using you, your emotions, and your ego as a tool to get what he wants. He has treated you as little more than a means to an end, which is dehumanizing and cruel.

Uninvolved or bored with you

Sometimes, the narcissist is there and nodding as though he is listening, but they are not actually seeming to care about what you are saying. You can tell that the narcissist's attention on you is begrudging at best, and they seem annoyed that they have to listen to you at all. The narcissist may respond to you shortly while using the tone that implies that he does not care about the situation at all.

This behavior tells you that you are unimportant. The narcissist has dehumanized you through not doing anything at all. He has made it clear that he does not value you with a few short words and the tone of his voice implying as much.

Emotional Blackmail

Emotional blackmail is another abuse tactic in which the narcissist attempts to manipulate you into whatever it is he wants from you. He typically takes advantage of your weaknesses or other things that you have told to him in confidence to get what he wants. It is typically so covert that most people do not realize it is happening at all, and when they may finally identify that they are being manipulated, they struggle to identify how it is happening or how to combat it.

There are three major parts to emotional blackmail: Fear, obligation, and guilt. Each of these gets weaponized against you to trick you into obeying. The narcissist is able to get these results without you ever suspect they are being used.

Emotional blackmail can use one, two, or three of these, and can be tweaked to serve the narcissist better. He will choose whatever is beneficial to him, typically erring in choosing the path that will be the least effort. The narcissist will have spent the first part of a relationship learning what makes his or her partner tick in an effort to figure out how best to manipulate the victim later on.

Fear

We all feel fear at one point or another. This is what motivates us to stay alive and protect ourselves—it is the body's natural alarm that signifies that something is not quite right and needs to be addressed. We do not necessarily have to be afraid of physical harm either. We can be afraid of loss, the unknown, or abandonment.

Nearly anything can become fear. The narcissist will identify what your fears are and threaten you with them. For example, if your biggest fear is losing your children, the narcissist may threaten to take them away and never let you see them again if you do not stay in line.

Obligation

An obligation is what we feel to those we see as being within our own community. We want to take care of those in our inner circles, and obligation is what motivates that. It enables the species to be successful, along with empathy. The narcissist understands this, though he feels no obligations himself, and he will prey upon other people's sense of obligation. The narcissistic parent may say that the adult child owes him after being brought up. The narcissistic spouse may play on "marital duties" or tell you that he would do what he is asking if the roles were reversed.

Guilt

Guilt is what is felt when we do not satisfy obligations. Narcissists use this as their safety net. If you do not do something that the narcissist has requested or implied you are obligated to do, he will then seek to make you feel guilty for doing so, hoping that the guilt will be enough to push you into doing it. If your sense of obligation to your narcissistic parent is not fulfilled, your parent may cry to you and say that you do not care after all he did for you, and he will tell you that he sacrificed everything to raise you in the hopes of guilting you into doing whatever it is he wants.

Gaslighting

Gaslighting involves the act of convincing someone else that their understanding of reality is skewed or inaccurate in some way. The narcissist is a master at gaslighting, and it is one of his most frequently wielded manipulative weapons. The narcissist will seek to make you doubt yourself, slowly at first, until you are so certain that you cannot be trusted that the narcissist is able to take control of everything. Because you may doubt yourself so much that you no longer trust yourself to make important decisions, you will rely more on your partner. This also makes you far more likely to stay in the relationship, as you will not trust that what you think happened actually did. You will listen when the narcissist downplays it or tells you that it was not what you think it was.

Typically, this starts out slowly, with the narcissist making your belief seem like a harmless mistake. For example, you may tell him that your car keys are on the key holder, and he will correct you a few minutes later, saying they were actually on the counter, even if they were, in fact, on the key holder. It escalates slowly from there until eventually, the victim believes anything the narcissist says.

Each incident of gaslighting will follow a specific pattern: Something happens. The narcissist either has a distorted view of what has happened, such as him being the victim in an argument that he started, or he creates a distorted view that will fit his narrative, even if he knows it is false. The narcissist then convinces the victim of his distorted truth. The victim then believes the narcissist.

Narcissists may try one of the following methods to gaslight you into submission:

- **Withholding:** The narcissist refuses to hear your side of things or pretends that your side of the story does not make sense.

- **Countering:** The narcissist directly counters or questions the victim's perception of what has happened, questioning if it is accurate.

- **Diverting:** The narcissist changes the subject and accuses the victim of misremembering.

- **Trivializing:** The narcissist makes the victim feel as though what the victim is saying or feeling is unimportant, or delegitimizes them.

- **Denying:** The narcissist feigns having forgotten what has happened or denies anything that the victim says, saying it is falsified or made up on purpose.

Love Bombing, Discarding, Devaluing, Hoovering

1

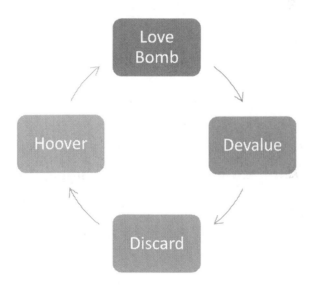

Love bombs

While love bombs may actually sound somewhat pleasant at first glance, they are a particularly insidious manipulation tactic. They seek to addict the victim to the narcissist by creating conditioning in which the victim associates the narcissist with good feelings. Just as a drug addict gets hooked to the euphoria the drugs he ingests causes, the narcissist will become the euphoric object to which the victim is attracted.

The narcissist will shower the victim in gifts, praises, love, attention, and anything else the victim's heart desires. He will likely provide anything the victim can think of, and will not think twice about it. He will push for the relationship to proceed in a typical romance movie whirlwind fashion and win the victim over through grand promises.

Devaluing

Eventually, however, the love bombs slow, then stop. The narcissist then decides to start chipping away at the victim's self-esteem through snide comments, making the victim feel unworthy of love, or even through outwardly calling the victim names. The entire purpose of this stage is to unsettle the victim and ensure that the victim decides to try to jump through hoops in order to get back into the narcissist's good graces. The victim wants nothing more than to be showered in love again, and the narcissist preys off of that.

Discarding

Eventually, not even the victim's attempts at trying to meet the narcissist's every whim are enough to keep him satisfied, and the narcissist decides to disappear altogether. He discards the victim, oftentimes without a word, leaving the victim in shock and wondering what had just happened. The victim does not understand how someone who had been so passionate before could suddenly lose all of that passion and become as cold as the narcissist.

The victim is likely to reach out in attempts of getting the narcissist back, and the narcissist thrives off of this. He loves being pursued, and it validates his own ego. He may remain silent a little while longer before moving on to the next stage.

Hoovering

Hoovering involves sucking the victim back up, much like a vacuum. Just when the victim has begun to accept that the narcissist is gone, the narcissist comes tearing back into the victim's life with promises of doing better. The narcissist will say anything to get the victim to agree to get back in line. If the victim decides to try again, which will most likely happen due to the desire to get back to the love bomb stage again, the relationship will repeat the cycle all over again, going through the love bomb, the devaluation, the discarding, and hoovering all over again.

Baiting

The narcissist, master of manipulation, frequently casts out bait to get his way. He will lull you into complacency, making you feel as though your relationship is stable and comfortable, only to bait you into inciting an argument. Oftentimes, the bait involves something you are sensitive about. The narcissist may know that you are sensitive about being cheated on in the past, for example, so the next time you are out, he may look at another person, intentionally appearing obviously interested in the other person. He may even go and flirt with the other person in an attempt to make you feel jealous.

When you inevitably call him out, he will deny having ever done anything like what you are insisting. He will say that he had no interest in the other person and turn it into an argument about your own insecurities. He has essentially tricked you into an argument, and when anyone asks, he will tell the world that you constantly accuse him of cheating when he has no interest in being anything other than a perfect partner.

This has allowed the narcissist to create a victim narrative after baiting you into acting irrationally, and he will use that cast bait any time he can. He wants to make you feel as though you are the irrational, abusive one.

Crossing Boundaries

While boundaries are healthy in every relationship, the narcissist sees them as a challenge. Any time the narcissist is asked not to cross a boundary, it becomes a sort of game to see just how far the narcissist can push to see what happens. He does not like boundaries and will cross them just to tell you that he does not respect them, or you.

If you tell him that you are not comfortable with certain behavior, for example, he may make it a point to insert that behavior in as much as he can, waiting to see your response. If you do not react in a way that tells him that the behavior is unacceptable, he will feel as though he has won a battle and gotten his way. If you call him out, he will say that you misunderstood his behavior and try other manipulation techniques to get you to believe that he was not intentionally stomping all over your boundary, and he will play the victim, as expected.

The narcissist sees boundaries as walls between him and what he wants, as boundaries make manipulation and control difficult. Even if you do try to enforce boundaries, expect the narcissist to make it a point to go about chipping at them, slowly at first, to try to get to any weaknesses or gaps in your boundaries in order to exploit them.

Defamation

Defamation of character typically involves the narcissist intentionally creating a dialogue in which you have been the problem in the relationship all along. Typically reserved for whenever a narcissist's target has cut off the narcissist, this is used in order to try to save face. The narcissist knows it will reflect poorly on him if he were to be broken up with and instead creates a narrative that says the opposite.

If you broke up with him because he was cheating on you, suddenly he is telling everyone in your area that you had cheated on him and broken his heart. If you broke up because he drank too much, he tells everyone in the area that you were drunk by 5 pm every single day. If he was simply inattentive and you desired more out of your relationship, he would declare that you neglected him constantly.

This is an attempt for the narcissist to once again become the victim in a situation. He wants to claim that everything that has happened was someone else's fault, and by saying that he had to leave the relationship because he was maltreated would make him the ultimate victim in the eyes of many in your area.

Violence

Narcissists, when they are unable to get their way through manipulation, do not shy away from physical abuse. Sometimes, the narcissist simply can no longer control his anger, particularly the toxic or closet narcissists, and he lashes out physically in an attempt to physically force you into submission. He may take away your phone to prevent you from calling for help, or break things to scare you, or he may even physically harm you.

The narcissist does not feel bad about hurting other people, and even if you are in a relationship with him, he sees nothing wrong with what he is doing. The narcissist only cares about getting his results, and if hitting you is the only thing that will work at the moment, then the narcissist will do it.

Isolation

Isolation is yet another commonly used tactic to manipulate the narcissist's victim into dependency. The narcissist will seek to be an all-consuming presence in the victim's life. He wants to be everything, leaving no room for other relationships. This ensures that the victim is always present to take care of whatever the narcissist wants whenever the need arises.

Typically, the narcissist may start by voicing displeasure with certain people around the victim, such as saying that he disapproves of your friends or family. He wants you to feel as though he will be unhappy if you continue to maintain a relationship with those other people. He will push it further by saying that you can only go hang out with them if he is present, typically due to some misguided, exaggerated fear that he says he has. For example, he may say that it is dangerous for you to spend time with a man, even though you are in a group of friends. He makes you feel like you have no choice but to let him come along, and when he gets his way in, he will make it clear that he is miserable. He will make those in the group with you hate him, and will try to make it so your friends stop inviting you to events, which they will do after a few iterations of him coming along and ruining your fun.

Eventually, he will burn the bridges to most, if not all, of your relationships, and keep you isolated away from everyone. He wants you to be all his, and he is not interested in sharing.

Part II

Dealing with Narcissistic Abuse

Chapter 4: Handling Narcissistic Abuse

Narcissists are not easy for anyone to handle, and even in the best of situations, dealing with narcissistic abuse is still tedious and annoying. There are always risks of abuse when associating with a narcissist, and ultimately, you have to take steps to mitigate or end the abuse if you want to protect yourself. The narcissist is opportunistic, and if you make yourself undesirable or difficult to manipulate, he will have no interest in doing so with you, instead preferring to move onto an easier target.

Cut-Off

Ultimately, the easiest way to deal with a narcissist is to cut him off entirely. If you have no relationship with the narcissist, the narcissist cannot manipulate you any further. Of course, cutting off someone as parasitic as the narcissist is not an easy feat by any means. The narcissist seeks to latch onto anyone around him and will use every skill in the book to stop someone from leaving him if he has decided to target someone.

If you decide that you want to cut off the narcissist, you will get the best results by telling the narcissist exactly once that you are permanently ending the relationship and that you have no interest in reconciling. You want to be as clear as possible, so he knows where you stand. Of course, he will not respect what you are saying, and he will attempt to worm his way back into your life, but you should still start by declaring the relationship over.

From there, your best bet is to prepare for the proverbial storm. The narcissist is going to unleash all of his anger upon you, attempting everything from guilting to threatening you back into submission. He wants you to be afraid of the consequences if you intend to end the relationship. He may stalk you, threaten you, vandalize your car, or attempt anything else that will motivate you to return to him just to make it all stop.

The reason for this is that the narcissist is going through an extinction burst. Think of a toddler who has been getting a bottle every time he has cried. He has this idea that life works a certain way, and that every time he cries, he is handed a bottle. He loves this bottle and often seeks it just for comfort. One day, his parents decide to wean him from the bottle altogether. He cries for the bottle, and his parents tell him "no." The toddler is shocked. He cannot comprehend that he is being denied something that has been given to him without fail for his entire life. He cries harder, hoping to get the bottle. If the parents have done their research, they understand that giving the bottle at this point will only encourage the temper tantrum and prolong the weaning process, so they stick to their guns and say no. The child continues to cry and cry, ramping it up and trying desperately to get the parents to give in. This may go on for days until the child, realizing that it is futile, gives up. He may try again a week or two later, but the attempt to get the bottle will be quite feeble, and he will not fight it too much. After being denied again, the child is considered weaned. He has accepted that he will not get the bottle any longer.

The narcissist behaves the same way. He has always been able to manipulate you into submission, and he seeks to do it again. When you refuse to give in, he throws a bigger tantrum, escalating and trying to scare you, until it peaks. He will eventually give up, though narcissists tend to be quite persistent. If you plan on cutting off the narcissist, ensure that you are prepared to weather the entire extinction burst, as if you find yourself giving in at some point, you are going to make things harder in the long run.

Timeout

Sometimes, cutting off the narcissist is not an option. Perhaps he is a family member, and you would prefer not to sever the relationship completely. If you find yourself feeling overwhelmed with the narcissist's antics, you can try a timeout. The purpose of the timeout is less about punishing the narcissist and more about taking time to yourself to regather your thoughts, regain your temper, and keep from doing something you will regret. You are taking some time to care for yourself to make sure that your mental health does not suffer. If you want to take a timeout from the narcissist, all you have to do is stop responding. You can tell the narcissist your intention if you want to, but you will probably just alert him to your act of withdrawing sooner than is absolutely necessary, which may just bring him bothering you sooner. You do not need to tell him how long you plan on distancing yourself, nor do you have to make that decision at this point in time. You can take as little or as long of a timeout as you desire, as it is for your own benefit.

Of course, the narcissist does not want you to consider your needs. He is likely to resist the idea of being put in a timeout, as he sees being abandoned and isolated as the ultimate affront. He is likely to go through an extinction burst period as well, threatening you, crying to you, attempting to guilt you, and pulling out any tactics he thinks may benefit him. He will likely turn himself into the victim, asking how you could do something like this to him, which is also an attempt to goad you into responding and therefore violating your own timeout. The key here is to stick to your guns and continue with the timeout, no matter how much he complains. If you do respond to him, all you have done is taught him that he can disrespect you and your boundaries with no consequence.

Low Contact

When a narcissist cannot be cut off, but you want to minimize contact to him, you can do what is called going low contact. In this case, you are minimizing any interactions you have with the narcissist, which effectively serves to create distance between yourself and the narcissist to shield you from manipulation. This is not always practical, as it is not likely to be very effective if you, for example, live with the narcissist and share a bedroom and living space. However, if you have a coworker or a distant family member that is narcissistic, you could try utilizing this method to create some distance.

When you go low contact with a narcissist, you are still open to seeing him, and you may interact with him in limited capacities, such as at family events or when work dictates it, but you keep things as impersonal as possible. You attempt to keep your distance emotionally in order not to give the narcissist any ammunition against you. You never answer any personal questions, instead of deflecting to something else. For example, if your great aunt Winifred is a horrible narcissist, but she goes to every family reunion, you would do your best to avoid her. You would see her at the reunion, and you would not be rude to her or outright ignore her, but you would seek to minimize your interactions with her. If she were to start talking to you, asking prying details about your marriage and your children, you could answer this with a short, "Those are none of your concern, aunt Winifred. Have you tried the rolls that Brenda brought to the potluck? They're incredibly fluffy. You should go try one."

In this case, you shut down her attempts to get information to use to blackmail or humiliate you with, and instead redirected to something else. The same concept can be applied at work, or anywhere else you find yourself running into someone far too nosy for their own good.

Grey Rock

If there is a narcissist you cannot cut out of your life, the grey rock method can help you. Sometimes, a narcissist has to be kept in your life for one reason or another. Perhaps you have decided that leaving a job to avoid the narcissist seems pointless, or maybe you are court-ordered to co-parent with a narcissistic ex. No matter the reason, the grey rock method can help you mitigate the damage from narcissistic abuse.

The grey rock method draws from the idea that no one pays attention to the rocks they pass on a trail when on a hike. If you are hiking, are you going to be looking at the average rocks all over the ground, or would you be looking at the trees, the sky, and the general wilderness as a whole? You would most likely pay attention to the entire forest, not thinking to consider the rocks as you can find rocks anywhere. There is nothing special, nor is there anything interesting, about a small rock on the side of the trail. Unless that rock is a gemstone, you are not likely to notice it. In this case, it is just a small grey rock, and it goes undetected.

You want to emulate the rock when dealing with a narcissist you cannot cut off. You essentially make yourself so boring, so unremarkable, and so utterly unresponsive to anything beyond the bare minimum that the narcissist gets bored and finds someone else to harass instead.

For example, imagine that your narcissistic ex with whom you co-parent a young daughter just sent you a text message that accuses you of withholding the child because you did not answer the phone when you were busy bathing her. The narcissist accuses you of parental alienation or of being a bad parent who does not recognize that children need mothers and fathers in their lives and sends a general rant about how awful of a parent you are. You should ignore everything about the message that is a direct attack. You do not even have to justify why you did not answer the phone when he called. Instead, just move on and allow your child to call back when she is free. You do not engage any time the narcissist attempts to goad a certain reaction from you.

Over time, the more you refuse to give the narcissist the response he is trying to get, the more distance you will notice between the two of you. He will eventually grow bored of trying, feeling as though you are no longer worth the effort, and move on to someone else.

Changing the Subject

Remember how when your great aunt Winifred tried to pry into your personal life a few pages ago? You changed the subject on her before she could get any valuable information from you. This tactic is great for use with a narcissist. Narcissists frequently attempt to pry for information they can use, and by changing the subject before answering, you can typically avoid the subject altogether.

When dealing with a known narcissist, one of the easiest ways to change the subject is to direct the conversation back to the narcissist. Narcissists love to talk about themselves, and he will likely revel in you asking a question about his most recent achievement at work that he has exaggerated to make seem more impressive than it actually is. He would love nothing more than to have a captive audience to his tale, and you would love nothing more than to keep from being pestered about your personal life. Win-win.

Manage Expectations

Ultimately, one of the biggest ways to keep from getting hurt by a narcissist is to manage your own expectations. You know that the narcissist has a personality disorder, and you know that personality disorder comes with certain symptoms or traits. Expecting the narcissist to behave narcissistically can prevent you from getting into all sorts of situations that could potentially be dangerous for you.

Just as you would exercise caution around a snake, dog, or other animals with the potential to hurt you, you should exercise caution around the narcissist. This does not excuse his behavior, nor does it mean you have to tolerate the behavior. What it does mean, though is that you recognize the narcissist's tendencies and you make sure to avoid situations in which you are sure the narcissist will fail. For example, if you know that the narcissist never bothers to be much of emotional support for others due to not really empathizing well with other people, do not look to him to be emotional support for you. You will be happier in general if you expect the narcissist to act like a narcissist so you can take the precautions necessary to avoid harm.

Set and Maintain Boundaries

Boundaries are quite important in society. They set lines in the sand between people that let other people know where people's hard limits are. When everyone recognizes the boundaries of those around them, everyone is happier. However, narcissists do not care about other people being happy, and they do not care about recognizing boundaries.

When you are setting a boundary, you should make sure that you always set and enforce a consequence for violating it. If you set a consequence and do not enforce it, the narcissist feels as though the consequence is optional and does not always apply. For example, imagine that you have set a boundary saying that you are not okay with the narcissist criticizing everything you do without a purpose. You tell the narcissist that if he feels the need to be overly critical all the time, you will put some distance between yourself and the narcissist and you can try the conversation at a future point in time.

The narcissist will likely poke at the boundary to see how much he can get away with. If he starts to voice something that is even slightly critical at all, you should tell him that you warned him about being so critical and walk away from the conversation. For every subsequent violation of your boundary, you should make the consequence more severe. Take a longer time apart to cool down, or keep your distance in general. This tells the narcissist that you are not willing to put up with such egregious disrespect and that you mean business when you are enforcing a boundary.

Depersonalize

Never take what the narcissist says or does personally. If you can avoid making it about you and instead recognize that it actually is a failure on the part of the narcissist, you will be far happier. Of course, this is easier said than done, but if you are able to avoid feeling insulted because the narcissist did something remotely narcissistic, you will be happier. Would you be insulted or offended if your dog stole a piece of ham that fell on the floor? Probably not. Would you be offended if a bird ate several of the berries growing in your garden? Probably not. Of course, both would be annoying, but you would not take it as a personal attack. You would recognize that both animals were simply acting in accordance with their nature. Apply that sort of concept to the narcissist as well, and you are likely to alleviate a lot of your stress.

Narcissists will almost always continue to behave narcissistically. This is not because they have a personal vendetta against you—it is simply in their nature to behave in such a way. You should not take the narcissist's manipulation any more personally than you would take a child calling you a dirty stink face for upsetting her when you told her she could not have any candy. When you learn to let go of the offense you feel, dealing with the narcissist becomes so much easier. You are able to see clearly because you are not being ruled by your emotions, and you can react appropriately.

Resist Arguments

Lastly, if you are finding yourself frequently interacting with a particularly argumentative narcissist, you should try to resist the urge to argue. This almost seems counterproductive, as oftentimes, silence is wrongfully taken as consent, but in this case, it is the easiest way to proceed. If the narcissist wants to goad you into an argument that he can use as a weapon later, you are better off disarming him through not giving him the argument at all, even if that means that you do not correct something he has said.

For example, imagine that your narcissistic friend has just told you that you messed up the food you were cooking again like you always do. She says it with a rough tone in her voice and while rolling her eyes, making her displeasure more than obvious. She is looking for an argument. You can shrug your shoulders and say, "Sorry about that," and avoid the argument altogether. By not trying to defend yourself, you just removed the weapon she was trying to arm herself with. She could not try to play the victim if you did not do anything that could potentially be seen as aggressive or abusive.

This tactic can be useful at disarming small arguments, but remember, you should always enforce your boundaries. This is a case of picking your battles. If you can avoid the argument, you should absolutely do so. However, if you need to defend yourself from what the narcissist has said, that is your prerogative. Even just ending some of the arguments, ensuring that the occur slightly less often, is likely to have an effect on your general experiences with the narcissist.

Chapter 5:

Avoiding Narcissistic Abuse

Ultimately, while dealing with narcissist abuse as it occurs is useful, being able to make yourself an undesirable target altogether is even better. Through following these various steps, you will be able to make yourself far less desirable as a victim than the narcissist would prefer. When you make it clear that you are unwilling to give the narcissist the source of supply that he craves, you are likely to be discarded altogether, which is the best care scenario with a narcissist. No longer in the narcissist's spotlight, you will be free to live your life without narcissistic abuse.

Keep Contact Minimized

The less contact you have with a narcissist, the less they can abuse you. If you know someone is an abuser, you should do everything in your power to have as little contact with the narcissist as possible. When you are able to avoid spending time with them, they cannot get any ammo against you. They cannot manipulate you; they cannot guilt you, and they cannot harass you. Of course, the narcissist can try smear campaigns, but that still requires at least some level of proximity. If the narcissist has never been around you, they are unlikely to be credible when trying to spread gossip. They need to have some general idea of the person you are, which they will need some degree of contact to discover.

The narcissist may try to bait you into contact by attempting to call you cold or frigid, hoping that you will be more willing to conform to social norms, but do not give in. It is just a trick meant to prey on the fear of being seen as rude that many people had instilled in them as children. This is just the narcissist grasping at straws and hoping that he can find something that sticks and works to manipulate you. You do not have to give in, nor do you owe the narcissist a pleasant conversation just because he called you rude.

Never Give in to Pressure or Demands

Narcissists are big on laying down the pressure. They, like an incessant child, will try again and again to get the same result, and they may eventually wear you down so much that you give in. This is exactly what the narcissist is banking on, so make it a point to avoid doing it! Never give in to the narcissist's pressure. Instead, remind yourself that insanity is doing the same thing over and over again while expecting a different result and remaining firm in your resolve.

Sometimes, it can help to think of yourself physically digging your heels in when the narcissist continues to harass you. By not giving in, the narcissist will eventually get the idea that you are inflexible and difficult to manipulate, therefore deeming you not worth the effort. If you had given in after the incessant demands, he would see that as a known breaking point and be willing to push well past that point in the future in order to get the result again. Remember that this behavior is no different than a child harassing you for ice cream, and refuse to give in. Keeping your cool and maintaining composure will likely be the most difficult part here, as well as having answers for the constant badgering. You can try shutting the narcissist down by saying, "Asked and answered," firmly, but emotionlessly after he tries pushing, and eventually just stop answering altogether. The narcissist will get the idea eventually, and your sanity will thank you.

Maintain your Values

The narcissist is likely to try to push you out of your comfort zone in the hopes of pushing you into doing things that he wants, even if you are uncomfortable with the requests. If you are uncomfortable doing something, such as being asked to steal something or forge a document for the narcissist, then it is acceptable for you to decline. Ultimately, your values, the integrity of your moral code, are more important than catering to the demands of a narcissist who has no regard for other people or their feelings. No matter how much the narcissist may push you, you should always refuse to do anything you are that uncomfortable with, especially if they violate your values or moral code.

Remember, the narcissist does not care much for social conventions, but that does not mean that you have to give up your own respect for them. When the narcissist insists, remember the previous step and refuse to give in. Remember to use the phrase, "Asked and answered" if he wants to keep harassing you in an attempt to bully you into doing his bidding. You will be far happier if you maintain your integrity, and the narcissist will likely go find someone else that is willing to do whatever he is asking. You once again would put yourself on the list of people that are too much of a hassle to manipulate, and the narcissist is not likely to continue harassing you in the future.

Avoid Face-to-Face Interaction

When you are forced to communicate with a narcissist, whether because you work with the narcissist or you are co-parenting with one, you should try to avoid interacting verbally or face to face if you can manage. Try to keep all communication written, as it is far more difficult to twist what is being said if it is right in front of you in black and white. You will be able to maintain your own composure as you will be able to take as long as you need to respond to the narcissist, so the narcissist cannot manipulate your emotions to get what he wants, and the narcissist cannot try to twist your words or insist you said something that you did not.

Particularly if you are co-parenting with a narcissist, there are several applications available that will record your communication in one place while also enabling you to keep a shared calendar for children and share documents that both parents will need or want, such as progress reports or bills for copays or deductibles for medical care.

Ultimately, it is next to impossible to remove all face to face interaction entirely, but you will be happier if you can at least minimize it. You will be able to respond easier, and you may even find that the narcissist is more formal and careful with a written communication as he does not want written record of his abusive tendencies and attempts at manipulating or coercing.

Mind Your Word Choice

Narcissists are very reactive. Saying something the wrong way can very quickly turn a situation that was meant to be calm into a screaming argument. Minding your wording with a narcissist is incredibly important. You want to word things in a way that there is no ambiguity and that the narcissist cannot twist. You also want to make sure you stay away from anything that could be seen as an attack or affront to the narcissist, as he is likely to react poorly to it.

If you need to have a conversation with the narcissist about something that has happened, for example, wording things that address your feelings in relation to what happened is far more likely to have a good ending than saying something that the narcissist may take as an attack and react to. For example, try using phrases like, "I feel like this could be done to make this even better," if you are trying to offer constructive criticism. The narcissist is less likely to take offense if you use "I" focused statements as opposed to "You" focused ones. However, be realistic here—Narcissists always find some way to turn themselves into the victim, even when the situation is entirely innocent.

Avoid Labeling or Judging

Along with minding how you phrase things, keep in mind that you want to be careful about the kinds of things you say. You should not say things that come across as judgmental, particularly when they are negative judgments. The narcissist will likely eat up any judgments that are positive, such as announcing that the cake that the narcissist made is delicious, and you love it more than any cake you have ever had. However, if the judgment is negative or perceived as negative, such as saying that the cake was pretty good, but the texture of the frosting seemed a little too thick and that maybe the narcissist should add just a touch more milk next time, the narcissist is not likely to respond well.

Likewise, labeling comments should be avoided altogether. Labeling statements are things such as, "You are great" or "That was awful." They are statements that say something is something else, essentially assigning a label. Negative labels toward people are typically things like, "You are stupid and useless," in which the other person is assigned the label of stupid and useless. The person is then synonymous with those labels in the statement. These can be quite hurtful. When dealing with the narcissist, avoid the temptation to say things such as, "You are so stubborn! Why are you so hardheaded?" or other things that label the narcissist as something else. He will not respond kindly to this, and you are more likely just to cause a worse argument than you could have had by saying, "I am done with this conversation," and walking away instead of dwelling on his stubbornness.

Avoid Confrontation When Possible

Sometimes, whatever the narcissist is saying or doing is not worth the argument that correcting it would cause. You may be better off letting the narcissist think he has won, and then not reacting any further to make him lose interest in you. While the narcissist loves people that are nonconfrontational, he likes people who will let them rule the situation. If you refuse to engage at all, the narcissist cannot trigger confrontation when it works well for him. This essentially makes dealing with you a waste of time in his book, and he is likely to seek someone else.

Remember, there is a difference between nonconfrontational and tactfully avoiding any confrontation that does not serve a purpose. Just because you refuse to engage in an argument sometimes does not mean that the narcissist can steamroll over you or take control of the situation. On the contrary, refusing to engage on your own terms keeps the power strictly in your own hands. The narcissist does not like when people refuse to allow him the power to do as he pleases, and if you maintain the power by not arguing on command, he is going to go elsewhere to someone who is easier to manipulate.

Recognize Your Worth—and Never Give it up

To avoid being victimized, and therefore avoid being targeted by the narcissist, you need to recognize your worth—your true worth. You should recognize that you are good enough, and you are deserving of love, happiness, success, and respect, whether the narcissist agrees or not. If you refuse to allow the narcissist to convince you otherwise, you are going to be able to avoid most of the narcissistic abuse. The narcissist seeks people who are willing to agree with him when he devalues you, and by knowing your worth, you are doing the exact opposite.

Just as you should always uphold your morals and values, you should always uphold your right to basic human decency. The narcissist is not likely to be attracted to you if you recognize your worth simply because you are not going to be as easy to manipulate.

Be Assertive

There is a fine line between assertive and aggressive. Assertive means that you are firm in your decisions, and you absolutely will uphold whatever you have decided upon. You are not willing to allow the narcissist to convince you of something you have decided you will not do simply because you know how to assert yourself. Being assertive means that you are defending your boundary, but without the anger. You are calm, rational, and fair about it, but you are not willing to let it slide.

When you are aggressive, you are emotional. The narcissist loves when people get emotional and will seek to take advantage of any time someone does display emotions. If you are aggressive in defending your boundaries, the narcissist will be able to play the victim, but if you are assertive, the narcissist has nothing to grasp at. He can hardly go crying to someone else that the big bully calmly but firmly insisted that the narcissist cannot hit him. That does not make sense, and no one would believe that he was a victim.

Do Not Protect the Narcissist

Ultimately, the best way to protect yourself and everyone else from narcissistic abuse is to make it a point to not protect the narcissist. Never try to explain away his insidious behaviors, and never try to justify what he has done. His behaviors are wrong, end of the story, and if you pretend, they are anything but wrong, you are enabling him to continue abusing. If you tell someone that he is pushy, but not that bad, they are more likely to be victimized by him when he comes and tries to bully them around simply because they have been told that other people tolerate him. Ultimately, people are quite likely to give in to peer pressure, and if you are telling other people that he is not bad, abusive, manipulative, or harmful, then you are making excuses for him, and you are enabling him.

This goes for when the narcissist tries to manipulate you as well—tell him clearly and firmly that you refuse to tolerate such behavior and refuse to engage further. You are making it clear to him that you are not making excuses to understand or justify the behavior and that you are unwilling to put up with it. He is not going to want to stick around someone who will not do mental gymnastics to avoid an uncomfortable social situation, and will instead seek someone else to bother that will be more willing to tolerate it.

Part III

Recovering from Narcissistic Abuse

Chapter 6: Stages of Recovery

Recovery from narcissistic abuse is a long, arduous journey, but once you reach the end, you will realize that you would not have it any other way. While the journey is difficult, you will discover a whole new world out there for you, in which you are free to do what you want without fear of being abused or manipulated. You will no longer have to cater to another person's every whim to avoid being hurt. You will no longer have to sacrifice yourself in order to better someone else. You can finally focus on *you* again. That may seem exhilarating right now—the idea of freedom. You can attain it if you are ready to begin the journey. Just know that this is a long road, and it is entirely normal to have setbacks sometimes. Be prepared for a journey that takes you months, or even years, depending on how much abuse you have endured during your life. What you can be assured of is that you are capable of healing.

As you heal, you will move through several stages before reaching the end. Each stage will involve you discovering new clarity on the situation you endured for far too long, and each stage will be difficult in its own way. Remember that it is okay to fear the future—most people do. It is okay to fear the unknown, and most people fear that as well. However, have faith in yourself that you can get yourself through this because you can.

Acknowledgment

The first stage of healing is acknowledgment. This begins when you have finally opened your eyes and realized that you do not want to live in this life anymore. You recognize that what is happening is wrong and you do not want to put up with it. You finally see that the narcissist, who up until this point you have vehemently defended any time anyone said so much as a single word of negativity toward him, is an abuser. You finally see that what he has been doing to you for the duration of your relationship is abuse.

This is the hardest step for any person to get through. This is where people usually freeze up and realize that they are afraid to move forward. Staying in denial, believing that they were deserving of the abuse was so much easier than accepting that they had been abused. This is a hard concept to wrap your head around, especially if you have always prided yourself on being smart or as someone who makes good choices. Rest assured, you can still be smart and still make good decisions, but still somehow get ensnared in the narcissist's trap.

Remember, the narcissist is a predator—he has been honing his skills for a lifetime to enable him to hunt what he wants, and he managed to trick you. This does not challenge your intelligence or your ability to make good decisions. If anything, you should applaud yourself for figuring out that the narcissist is abusive. You should celebrate that you have made the decision to break free from his abuse and move forward in life. You have snapped yourself out of your denial, and that takes strength, intelligence, and courage.

You may have been victimized, but that does not mean you are weak. In acknowledging that you were a victim to the abuse, you are declaring that you are ready to move on. This is the first step of removing the blame of what has happened to you and assigning it where it belongs—on the narcissist.

You did not deserve what the narcissist did, and you have acknowledged this at this stage.

You did not ask to be abused, and you acknowledge this as well.

You did not ask to be a victim, and you did not deserve it. Say that to yourself in moments of weakness: "I did not ask for this, nor did I deserve this." Say it so often that you have no choice but to believe it any time that you start to feel doubt.

Ultimately, reaching the stage of acknowledgment means you are free of the blame, guilt, and shame the narcissist assigned to you. You acknowledge what has happened, and you are ready to take action.

Determination

The second step to healing from narcissistic abuse is called determination. When you reach the stage of determination, you are ready to take action. You have removed your blinders in the stage of acknowledgment, and you are ready to fix all of the wrongs you have identified.

When you are determined to heal, you are ready to start making the action plan; you will need to escape the abuse. You are able to separate yourself from the narcissist and begin identifying what you will need. You will be able to follow the steps on the action plan.

You will gather up everything you need, and with your ducks all nicely in a row behind you, you will be able to finally gather the strength to break free. You do this at this stage. You finally escape the narcissist, and your sheer determination for a better life keeps you away when the narcissist desperately tries to get you back in line.

Your determination becomes your shield and your sword. The narcissist tries to hoover you back in, and your determination to be your own person keeps you resolute. You recognize that you deserve so much more, and you are willing to fight for it. Your determination to be free enables you to do so much more than you ever thought you were capable of.

You know that at this point, you cannot turn back. Just like someone who has started turning only to realize that he has to speed up in order to avoid a collision while driving, you have to commit to the changes you are making or risk everything. This could be your only chance, and freedom is within your grasp if you just keep going. Put your foot on the pedal and race forward, no matter how tempted you might be to freeze or slam on the brakes in hopes of avoiding the other car.

It is difficult to remain in this stage for long, as you very quickly might find yourself lost, unsure of yourself, and alone. You may quickly begin to fall into old habits, in which you blame yourself, or you feel that sense of guilt at abandoning the narcissist creeping into your mind, poisoning your thoughts, and drawing from your determination to survive and thrive. This new, determined sense of self can be frightening to you once the initial inertia of escaping begins to wear away. This is where you begin to doubt yourself, and worry that you have made the wrong choice, or that you were wrong to see abuse there in the first place.

Remember to trust your instincts. The doubt nagging in the back of your mind is what the narcissist wants—it is what tethers you to the narcissist and keeps you willing to go back to him. It is the chain that the narcissist tugs, expecting you to come back obediently. You can free yourself from it if you resist. The longer you keep yourself firm in this stage, the more comfortable your new self, filled with the determination for a better life, will become.

You will begin to recognize that your newly enforced boundaries, your insistence to be free of abuse and manipulation, is a valid one. You will no longer allow yourself to be a victim of abuse, and as you become comfortable in this decision to keep yourself free of abuse, you will recognize it is a powerful one. You finally have discovered your power, your ability to be free and control your own life. You have taken back that power that the narcissist stole away from you, and you will be able to remove the chains that have kept you shackled for far too long. You feel like yourself for the first time in a very long time, and you are *free.*

Compassion

After finally escaping from the abusive, tyrannical rule of the narcissist, you finally have discovered your own power. You are able to view your situation with compassion for yourself. You are able to tell yourself that you did not deserve what you faced, and mean it. You are able to feel compassion for those who have suffered at the hands of narcissists elsewhere, understanding the difficult journey they went through to free themselves, as well as understanding how those who are not yet able to make the leap to freedom themselves are feeling.

As someone who has escaped abuse, you have finally reached the stage in which you no longer feel as though you are constantly being interrogated. You no longer feel the need to explain what you are doing to other people or justify every single decision you make. You no longer have to answer to other people, and you revel in this stage. You also recognize the autonomy of others. You finally reach the point of no longer having to apologize for every little mistake, no matter how innocuous, and you recognize that other people also will inevitably make mistakes. You know that making mistakes is a normal part of life, and you recognize that you have to allow other people to be accountable for their own mistakes—even the narcissist who abused you. You no longer feel the need to take on the burden of shielding other people from consequences, and you no longer feel as though you have to make it a point to fix everyone else's mistakes as they occur. You are finally able to see that you are not responsible for everything that goes wrong, and even in a relationship with someone else, you are not responsible for their behaviors.

Most importantly, you have reached a point in which you can love yourself. You have forgiven yourself for the abuse you have endured and for not seeing it sooner. You no longer hold the abuse against yourself and feel compassion for yourself, despite the fact that you may be able to identify a thousand times at which you should have seen that the relationship was toxic. You forgive yourself for falling for the narcissist's traps, and you no longer blame yourself for doing so. This is perhaps more freeing than actually escaping, as you finally let go of the last little bit of control the narcissist's abuse held over you for so long. You finally treat yourself with the kindness and compassion you deserve.

At this point, you are free to live a life free of the pain, and you will be able to treat yourself kindly when you do inevitably make mistakes. You will not hold it against yourself, nor will you belittle or demean yourself when you slip up. Even meeting someone who triggers your initial responses that the narcissist installed within you is not enough to entirely derail you. You no longer go into a panic as you feel the familiar guilt and obligation sneaking up on you, whispering lies into your mind. Instead, you choose to address it with a sense of quiet calmness, in which you attempt to identify why you reacted the way you did. Instead of being afraid and angry, you see it as an opportunity to learn and compassionately better yourself. You know that you can trust yourself to keep yourself safe and that peace of mind is absolutely invaluable.

At this stage, you are finally healed enough to begin engaging in relationships again. You have worked on yourself and your problems, and you are in control of who you are and what you will expose yourself to. You are stronger than ever before—a survivor who fought for freedom and won—and you will rely on that strength to keep you afloat as you once again begin to open yourself up to the idea of a relationship with someone else. You know what to look for and what to avoid, and you know how to recognize when your old tendencies are arising. You are able to recognize your own needs, your own boundaries, and you know exactly what you bring to the table in a relationship. You are finally ready to find real love—love that is healthy, freeing, and that will make you into a far better person than you ever imagined you could be.

Congratulations and celebrations are in order once this stage has been achieved. This is when you can finally breathe and know that you are truly safe.

Modeling for Others

Finally, you reach the final stage on your journey: Becoming a model. You are able to model for others the behaviors you have learned. You have learned so much throughout your journey with the narcissist, and at this stage, you are able to teach everything you have gotten from your experiences to those around you. The one bright side to the abuse, you may realize at this stage, is that it has prepared you to help those around you who are suffering the way you have before.

At this stage, you have developed compassion. You have changed as a person in more ways than you thought were possible, and you can begin using those changes to help others. You acknowledge at this point that you are not attracted to the abusers. The abuser's tactics no longer seem appealing to you, and you no longer care to be around those with a propensity to abuse others. You are, however, attracted to those who are stuck in abusive relationships. You are able to see them, feel compassionately for them, but not feel the need to rush in to save them. This is the key point here—you cannot run in and preach to them to tell them how to fix themselves or get what they need to better themselves. You have to approach them carefully and cautiously, and you can teach them through modeling your own behaviors.

People around you, you have learned, suddenly treat you with respect. They see you, someone who was once a battered individual, who is now a powerful, compassionate survivor who fought for freedom. When people, particularly abuse victims, ask you how you survived, you are willing to tell them your story, but you are careful never to tell them what they have to do.

You tell them the tales of acknowledging your abuse, and that moment when the clarity came to you, and you truly opened your eyes. You tell them of how desperately you worked to break free of the narcissist, and just how determined you were to be free and happy. You tell them about how difficult the journey was, but that you would never have it any other way, and you tell them that at this point, you are happy to help others that ask for help as well.

At this point, you show the abuse victim all the ways you respect yourself. They see it in the way you do not allow other people to take advantage of your goodwill at the store when they try to weasel their way in front of you in line. They see it when you actively call out the way someone at the park wronged you, in a calm, but firm manner. They see it when you refuse to let someone disrespect you or call you names without calling it out. They see it when you resist the urge to fall back into old ways.

The abuse victims around you see you surviving, living a life they can only dream of at this stage, and they are inspired. They want to emulate you, and you do your best to model the person they will have to be to break free. You do this without ever telling them what to do or how to do it—you allow it all to be their own decisions, as you understand better than anyone that the abuse victim will never escape before he or she is ready.

At this point, you have made it through it all. You have gone from the battered victim, too afraid to so much as stick a single toe out of line into a beautiful person with a true inner strength that those around you admire. You have become an admirable person. Like charcoal, you have endured intense pressures from all sides, and what came out was a beautiful diamond, and at this point, everyone can see how you shine. They see you shining, and they respect you and everything you have gone through.

This process was not overnight or even during the course of a few weeks. Remember, that to finally make it to the other side and be fully healed can take years. However, it is a process that will leave you a far better person than you ever thought you could be. Though the process may seem daunting now, remember that you never know how strong you are until necessity forces you to act. If you are ready to end the narcissist's abuse and free yourself, take the leap and necessity will let your truest self shine through. With a little faith in yourself, you can, and will, survive. You, too, have a diamond within you that will come out under pressure, so long as you take the plunge, run with the determination guiding you, and reach the compassion at the other end.

Chapter 7:

How to Heal from Narcissistic Abuse

When you are attempting to heal from the narcissist after escaping, somewhere during the determination stage, you will need to find ways to take care of yourself. You need to heal all of the wounds that the narcissist's abuse left behind in order to become the person you are meant to be. Healing can be incredibly difficult if left to your own devices, and you may even feel tempted to move on without ever addressing the harm you endured. However, it is essential. You will never truly heal if you leave the wounds to fester and worsen. Your sense of self, your happiness, and you, yourself, will slowly wither away if you do not treat the wounds. Just as you know, you must treat a physical wound; you must care for your mental and emotional wounds as well. Take the time to really absorb the methods of healing from abuse, and really put effort into bettering yourself. You will feel so much relief after you have taken the time to heal.

Remember, running away or putting your head in the sand and pretending that you are fine is what the narcissist taught you to do. No matter how tempting it may be to try to grit your teeth and move on, you need to address your injuries. In moments of weakness, remind yourself that you only want to do what is familiar, but doing so will not help or benefit you. It is simply falling back to old ways that can lead to a further setback, and potentially send you spiraling back to the narcissist. Only by healing all of the wounds can you truly remove all of the chains the narcissist has installed and really free yourself.

Self-Care

One of the easiest ways, in theory, to help heal yourself is to engage in self-care. Self-care can be difficult for even those with healthy minds, who are happy with themselves and do not have some serious healing to do. It is easy to get caught up in the bustle of life and give up the self-care time in favor of doing something else, but it is important to engage in.

Self-care, at its core, is taking care of yourself. You are making your physical and mental wellbeing a priority for yourself, and you are not ashamed of doing so. Particularly for the victims of narcissistic abuse, who have internalized that their needs are met last, this can be difficult, but it is an important skill to learn. The easiest way to engage in self-care is to create a routine in which you have several things that you do regularly in order to create good habits. If you are unsure where to start with self-care, here are several ideas of ways to start your self-care routine.

- **Good sleep hygiene:** Make sure you are going to sleep at the same time every night and pay attention to things that could make sleeping difficult, such as having a television in your room that keeps you awake or using your phone in the dark in bed. Keep the bedroom just for sleep!

- **Eat healthy food:** Make it a point to nourish your body to keep it physically healthy. Your gut and your mind are believed to be linked, and if you can keep your gut healthy, you will likely find your mental health improvements as well.

- **Exercise daily:** Exercise is not just good for the body—the mind needs it as well. Make it a point to take at least thirty minutes a day to exercise, whether it is a fitness class, time at the gym, or even just a stroll through the park. Just make sure that stroll gets your heart rate up!

- **Prioritize self-care:** The easiest way to engage in self-care is to prioritize self-care. Make sure that you guard the times you set aside for caring for yourself and treat them as precious. You deserve that time for your own well-being.

- **Take a trip:** Sometimes, taking a weekend vacation away from the bustle of work, friends, and the city can be incredibly refreshing. This works even better if you disconnect for a while and just let yourself enjoy your own presence. Keep your phone off, and enjoy your own company for a bit!

- **Take breaks often:** Mental health breaks are necessary to function effectively. Without them, you risk burning out and otherwise struggling to meet your responsibilities without being utterly miserable. Your breaks could even be simple five-minute breaks outside every couple of hours when working. Your sanity will definitely thank you for it.

- **Caring for a pet:** Pets bring an awful lot to our lives, even with the responsibilities that come with them. By having a pet, you encourage a relationship with something that is unconditional, lacking judgment, and can even lower your blood pressure. Dogs, in particular, are so good for self-care and healing that even PTSD sufferers have adapted them as service animals to help with mental health!

- **Staying organized:** If you are organized, you are less likely to stress out about forgetting something or how to fit everything in. Even something as simple as implementing a calendar or planner can benefit your mental health immensely.

- **Cook at home:** Along with eating healthily, cooking your own food can be surprisingly therapeutic. There is just something about taking raw ingredients, preparing them, and creating something nourishing and delicious from them that is so satisfying! Cook at home often to reap the benefits.

- **Read:** Read often. Not only is it good for your brain, but there is also a world of knowledge out there. You could even read a book about learning self-care! Even if the books you read are fiction, you can still benefit from reading. It keeps your mind stimulated and will help keep you healthier.

- **Learn a new skill:** Learning something new can help you raise your own self-esteem. At finally learning to do something new, you are likely to feel proud of yourself, which is great! Try learning something new, especially if it is something that has always interested you.

Compassion

As there is even an entire stage in the healing process called compassion, it comes as no surprise that it plays a part in healing from your abuse. Remember to have the compassion for yourself to acknowledge that you did not deserve the abuse you endured, and to recognize that making mistakes is okay.

Oftentimes, victims of narcissistic abuse struggle to be compassionate or patient with themselves—they feel as though they are underserving of that compassion, even if they would tell anyone else in their shoes that it is okay and that compassion is necessary. Even little things can set off a victim of abuse, such as spilling a glass of milk. If you have endured abuse, you may tell yourself that you are stupid for making such a simple mistake, and you may even belittle yourself, calling yourself a klutz and worthless.

The problem is, those are not your words—they are the narcissists. Spilling a glass of milk is not a big deal in the grand scheme of things. In terms of a mistake, it is harmless. Even if the glass shattered, no one died. There was no irreparable damage to anything other than a glass, that most likely does not have some immense value anyway.

Remember to regard yourself with the same compassion you have always had for others. You deserve it just as much as the people you treat with that compassion and directing some of that inward does not take away from anyone else either. The compassion and willingness to forgive yourself will go a long way.

That compassion should also come with patience. Recognize that it will take a significant amount of time for yourself to heal from the narcissist's abuse, but that does not invalidate you. That does not make you less valuable, and it does not say anything about your worth. It simply means that you are a human and you are likely to have roadblocks from time to time. Just because you trip and fall and make a mistake does not mean you should berate yourself or make yourself feel worse.

Allow Yourself Time to Grieve Properly

Grief is a natural part of living, in which people cope with loss. Typically, grief is reserved for people who have lost a close family member or friend, but as you go through the stages of separating yourself from an abusive relationship, you go through a similar process. This is because, particularly when involved with a narcissist, you *have* lost someone. You have lost the person you thought the narcissist was. Remember how the narcissist used a persona to draw you in—you fell in love with the narcissist's mask. You initially loved someone who turned out to be a figment of your abuser's imagination. However, the process of watching the narcissist morph from a perfect lover into a monster is devastating. It is not unlike watching someone fade away from a terminal illness, slowly losing him—but when you lose the narcissist's persona, you are left with a monster wearing your loved one's face as a constant reminder of what you lost.

When you met the narcissist for the first time, you saw someone charming, charismatic, friendly, and likely every single thing you have ever wanted. You essentially saw your soulmate standing in front of you, and over time, your soulmate faded away. First, the person you trusted with everything started to hurt you, a little at first, until the abuse was nearly constant. You were left, dismayed how someone you loved so deeply, who you thought loved you just as passionately, could suddenly shift into a monster, but he did. This is just as profound of a loss, even if you are losing the idea of a person. You still lost someone that you loved, and you should not minimize that. Grief comes in five stages: denial, anger, bargaining, depression, and acceptance.

Denial	• Immediately after the event • Shock, numbness
Anger	• Everything feels unfair • Desire for justice
Bargaining	• Desperation • Willing to do anything to go bac
Depression	• Realization of permanence • Withdrawing from world
Acceptance	• Healing • Accepting reality for what it is

Denial

When you get to denial, you want to deny that anything has happened. This was when you were ensnared by the narcissist, entirely convinced that the abuse was not as bad as it actually was. You denied that the person you loved was gone. After all, how could he be gone when you can see his face right there? You hold onto hope that the person you thought the narcissist was is still in there somewhere, and you make excuses. You may say that the narcissist was not so bad, or try to convince yourself that you are willing to stay behind because at least you get to see your loved one's face looking back at you through the abuse. You attempt to convince yourself that things will be okay. This is where you were before you reached the acknowledgment stage of healing. You refused to recognize the abuse for what it was.

Anger

Eventually, your denial gives in to anger. Your eyes are opened, and you finally want to break free. At this stage, you want to escape at all costs, telling yourself that you do not deserve this abuse. You feel angry at the narcissist for convincing you to stay with him, and for convincing you that the abuse is acceptable or normal. You feel angry that the person you loved is gone, or never existed in the first place. You feel betrayed and manipulated— because you were. The narcissist played a dirty trick on you, and you fell for it. More than anything, though, you feel angry at yourself for falling for it all. You tell yourself that you should have known better and you also push the blame onto yourself, even if you do not deserve it. You desperately want for the person you love to come back somehow, and you want the narcissist to pay for what he did to you. This is likely the stage in which you flee from the narcissist's abuse, no longer willing to put up with it anymore.

Bargaining

When you reach the bargaining stage, you are willing to give anything to return to the way things were before. You tell yourself that you will do whatever it takes to have the narcissist's persona back, whether it is putting up with the narcissist's abuse or anything else. At this stage, you are grappling with the permanence of the situation and are desperate for a sign that reality is not what it may seem. If you are religious, you may pray to your god to fix things, or that you will be more devout if your god can somehow give you a miracle and bring your loved one back to you without the narcissist. You promise to do anything that comes to mind, but of course, it does not work because your loved one was never a real, living person.

Depression

Soon after, you come to the realization of the permanence of the current situation. You see that you will never get your love back, and you fall into a depression. You are beside yourself that the person is gone and you are so miserable and unhappy with it that you stop feeling anything at all. You essentially turn off your feelings, instead of staying in self-pity. You recognize the futility of it all and wonder why you should even bother continuing with anything. Life feels hopeless, and you wonder if even the narcissist would be a better alternative than this hell alone. You miss the narcissist's persona so much it hurts, and the idea of never seeing that person you loved again is so overwhelming that you struggle to cope.

Acceptance

Eventually, you finally reach the stage of acceptance. Here, you finally see the light again. You recognize that the narcissist tricked you, but you also recognize that things will be okay. You still love the persona that you originally fell for, but you recognize that he was nothing but an attempt to manipulate you into falling for the narcissist. You see it for the weapon it was, and you accept letting it go. At this point, you seek to move forward, and you allow yourself to find enjoyment in other things and realize that what happened was not the end of the world and that you are open to the idea of finding real love again in the future.

Develop Support Networks

Recognizing that you cannot get through this process alone is probably one of the most indicative of whether you will be able to escape the narcissist's abuse. You need the support of other people to be there for you in moments of weakness, and when you feel like you can no longer go on without the narcissist. Having people, you can talk to and trust to help guide you makes you far more likely to make it through without going back to the narcissist for further abuse. Your support network can take many forms, but most of the time, it is built upon a foundation of four groups of people: Friends, family, support groups, and a therapist, if you have one.

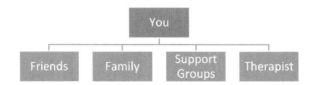

Friends

Friends will be there for you through thick and thin, and even if the narcissist has managed to isolate you from many of them, if you were to send a message to some of your closest friends from before the abuse, you would likely be surprised about how many of them are relieved and thrilled to hear from you. They may share that they have been waiting for you to contact them for ages and that they were always so concerned for you. Your friends will likely make up the bulk of your support group. These are people who will meet up with you on a bad day to watch movies and binge eat cartons of ice cream, or will let you rant about just how betrayed you feel by the narcissist. They will gladly be there for you and simply enjoy being in your presence in general. If you do not have friends, you should try to make some. There are many different ways you can do so, such as going to classes to learn new skills or groups you can join with people who share your interests. Especially with the internet at your disposal, you can likely google any hobby of yours and the city you live in, and be surprised to find groups of like-minded individuals that would probably be thrilled to have you if you contacted them and asked to join.

Family

Your family will likely be there for you if you ask for more serious help, such as needing money, a place to stay, or general support while trying to escape. Especially if you are escaping with children, your own family is a fantastic place to start. Your family only wants what is best for you, and as your friends, you may be surprised to hear that many of your family members had suspected abuse for a long time. They will also likely be relieved at you leaving, and you can frequently find plenty of support from these people.

Support groups

Support groups are particularly useful when you need someone that understands what you are going through more so than just having a general idea of how you felt. You can typically find support groups for narcissistic abuse survivors by searching online, both in your own area and online. There are several different forums and boards of people who get together to discuss their abuse, and you will likely be able to find other people that have gone through almost exactly what you have. The people that will understand the intensity of the abuse, the way the narcissist so thoroughly manages to break people down, and how hard it is to leave are the ones who have gone through it before and know it out of the experience.

When you find a support group that clicks for you, you will be able to see people at all stages of healing. You will see people who have more or less fully recovered and are there, supporting other people through their journeys toward healing, and others who may have just left, or have been considering leaving that are trying to learn what to do. This can be particularly useful, as you can look at other people who are further along than you are for inspiration. You can ask for advice, talk to people who have been where you are, and even just enjoy a conversation with someone who knows what you have gone through. Ultimately, this can be an incredibly insightful experience, and you will almost always get something good out of browsing through these forums or meeting up with other survivors. What will be clear when you do this, however, is that you are not alone by any means. Many, many people have fallen victim to the narcissist, and unfortunately, many more will as well. At the very least, there are several safe spaces on the internet and in person where the survivors of narcissistic abuse can come together to support each other toward healing and bettering themselves.

Therapist

A therapist can be particularly useful in helping heal as well. While you will have a professional relationship with a therapist as opposed to a friendship, you will be able to talk to the therapist to help you deal with difficult feelings or to deal with things that you are struggling to handle. The therapist, though optional, is always a fantastic choice when recovering from abuse if you can make it happen.

Creating Healthy Outlets

When you have suffered through narcissistic abuse, you have probably developed some pretty toxic thoughts and feelings yourself. Many of these come from what is likely a tendency toward being empathetic, as that is one of the things the narcissist desires most, and you absorbed the narcissist's toxic feelings. Empaths are particularly prone to internalizing the feelings and tendencies of those around them, and the tendencies of the narcissist can be particularly toxic to the empath.

One of the best things to do when you have internalized all of that negativity is finding a creative, healthy outlet for it. You should seek out some sort of way to eliminate the toxicity from you, whether through art, music, learning, taking classes, or anything else that appeals to you. Exercising is a common tactic used, in which you literally sweat out the negativity. The important part here is that you manage to eliminate it in some way and that you feel better after you have finished whatever you have chosen to do. Over time, you will release all of the pent-up negativity, and you will begin to feel much better about yourself.

Therapy

Therapy can guide you toward healing as well. As briefly touched upon, a therapist is one of the greatest favors you can do for yourself. There are very few people in this world who would not benefit from therapy, and the likelihood of one of them being you is incredibly slim. The sooner you start it, the sooner you will start seeing results. There are several different kinds of therapy that could be useful for a victim of narcissistic abuse, and through therapy, you would be able to learn valuable skills, such as how to cope with the trauma left behind, understanding what made you vulnerable to the narcissist in the first place, and how to solve all of the problems that come with all of the emotions you feel whirling around within you.

If therapy is something that sounds like it would benefit you, try speaking to your primary care doctor for a referral, or seek out recommendations local to your area online. Even if the cost is an issue, there are plenty that will help you on a sliding scale, as well as online options that may be more affordable for you.

Chapter 8:

How to Move on From the Narcissist

Ultimately, once you have escaped and begun to heal from the narcissist, you may be wondering how do you ever fully move on from the narcissist, particularly after he so thoroughly won your heart? It is definitely not an easy task, but if you have made it this far, you can do it. Moving on from the narcissist involves disengaging from the narcissist, practicing mindfulness, and bettering yourself. Through these skills, you will be able to distance yourself from the narcissist further, understand your feelings when you want to go back, and you can find a constructive way to use your feelings toward the narcissist.

With affirmations, you will have a tool in your back pocket to help you remember your value and what you want out of life.

Disengaging from the Narcissist

Disengaging from the narcissist will involve going through various stages, much like grieving. This is your process of letting go of the narcissist and recognizing that the relationship is ruined and needs to be ended permanently. Though easier said than done, disengaging and detaching from the narcissist is crucial to healing. Similar to the stages of grief, you will go through three distinct stages when you are attempting to disengage from the narcissist before finally reaching stage 4: freedom.

Stage 1: Refusing to take the blame

In stage 1, you refuse to allow yourself to be blamed for anything that happened. You tell yourself that you did not deserve what the narcissist did, and even though you may have ended the relationship, it was not you that degraded the relationship to the point that it had to be ended. This stage involves you recognizing that the narcissist will never give you what you deserved in the relationship. The narcissist will never be the partner you wanted him to be, and you recognize that. You acknowledge that the narcissist is flawed beyond your own ability to repair someone and that his destructive nature is not yours to manage, nor is it something that can be forced upon you. The narcissist becomes someone that you may love still, but you recognize the truth in the situation and that the relationship has to end for everyone's sake.

Stage 2: Anger and resentment

At stage 2, you realize that all of the hope you had for the relationship and the narcissist is being replaced. At this stage, you are angry. You see that the narcissist is not the person you wanted, and you begin to resent him. Even if you still have feelings at this stage, you are not likely to act upon them. Your eyes have been opened to the truth, and you refuse to allow the relationship to consume you any longer. At this stage, you no longer care about the manipulation the narcissist has likely been slinging at you to try to get you back. You really recognize that you deserve better than to be treated poorly or with disrespect. You feel the need to stand up for yourself and better yourself. You want to live a life of happiness, not one in which your sole duty is to provide someone else with the happiness you have been deprived of feeling for so long.

Stage 3: Detaching and setting yourself free

When you finally hit stage 3, you are finally detaching. The very sight of the narcissist or the mere mention of his name could be enough to make you feel sick to your stomach, and you realize that the love you had for him once upon a time has faded away. You have instead worked on bettering yourself. If you have been going to a therapist or been interacting with a support group, you are beginning to take their advice more frequently and realize that it works. You are far more concerned with getting what you want and need than worrying about the narcissist. You make your decisions based on what is best for you as opposed to anyone else, and for the first time in a long time, you can practically taste freedom.

Stage 4: Freedom

At this point, you are finally free. You no longer allow the narcissist to have any sway on you and you have likely cut all contact with him. You have completely and utterly separated yourself from the narcissist, and you could never feel better. Your freedom was earned through metaphorical, and quite possibly literal, blood, sweat, and tears, and you plan on enjoying it, no matter what the narcissist has to say about it.

Practicing Mindfulness

Mindfulness, at its simplest, is the idea that, when engulfed in chaos and strong emotions, you are able to take a moment to detach from the situation at hand and observe what is happening from a rational perspective. You sort of retreat within yourself to reflect on how you are feeling and why you are feeling the way you are in the hopes of finding answers that can help you better cope with what is bothering you.

This is a particularly useful way to identify any emotional triggers, those things in the outside world that automatically trigger you to feel everything the narcissist has programmed you to feel. There are undoubtedly some left in you after a relationship with a narcissist, but learning them all can take plenty of time and patience. When you want to practice mindfulness, you want to fully understand why you are responding the way you are.

This is a fantastic skill for anyone to have, as mindfulness can aid in controlling emotional outbursts, as well as help lessen stress. It is an incredibly healthy coping mechanism and is absolutely valuable to learn. Mindfulness involves five steps that will allow you to achieve the state of mindfulness. This state is a state of quiet, internal attentiveness. When you are first learning mindfulness, it is best to do so in periods of calmness to master the art before eventually beginning to use it when tensions run high.

Sit down

Step 1 in mindfulness is sitting down or identifying a quiet place in which you can quietly and safely focus on your breathing. Anywhere is acceptable, so long as you can focus and you are comfortable, so maybe try to find a quiet corner in your home, or underneath a tree in your yard. The important part here is that you need to be calm and relaxed wherever you choose.

Choose a time

With the goal in mind, choose how long you are willing to dedicate to your first few attempts at mindfulness. Typically, you are better off starting with a shorter period at first and slowly working your way up to longer ones. Perhaps, for your first time, set a goal of 5 minutes of mindfulness.

Pay attention to your body

Choose a comfortable position and really focus on your body. You want to choose a position in which you feel stable and relaxed, and that will be comfortable for the duration of your mindfulness. Once you have settled in, really start to focus on your body. Attempt to feel every part of yourself, starting at the tips of your toes and slowly working your way up to the top of your head. You should do this slowly as if you were mentally scanning yourself. Pay attention to any areas that are particularly tense and try to relax them.

Breathe

Focus on your breathing. Take one breath in and try to follow the feeling of it all the way into your lungs, holding it there before exhaling, and repeating. Make sure your breaths are deep, cleansing breaths, and really focus on each one.

Keep your mind on track

Any time you feel your mind wandering, quietly put it back on your breathing without judging yourself. Remember how you are supposed to feel compassionate about yourself? This is a good place to start! Particularly, in the beginning, it is easy to get distracted, and that is nothing to be ashamed of. Just regroup and continue.

After completing all the steps, you should feel far more relaxed than when you started. This can be a fantastic tool to use to unwind after a busy or stressful day, or when you feel your temper rising. As you master being able to call yourself to mindfulness when calm, you can begin using it as a coping mechanism when you feel frustrated or stressed out, or any time you start to debate whether returning to the narcissist would really be too bad. Oftentimes, those insecurities are tied to some sort of physical distress, and you should try to let them go as best as you can.

Another trick for mindfulness that some people find works well, particularly when emotions are running high is the 5-4-3-2-1 rule. In this technique, you seek to identify things around you with your various senses, engaging them instead of allowing your negative emotion to consume you, and when you focus on yourself again, you are better able to manage your own reactions in the future.

Sight

First, start by identifying five things around you that you can see. Be as descriptive as possible with yourself if you can be. Perhaps you see a blue ball with a woven texture on the ground, smooth, clear glass on the table next to you, and a sky the color of a clear blue ocean that you dream about vacationing to see. When you have identified five things to yourself, you are ready to move on to your next sense

Touch

Next, focus on your sense of touch. Notice four different things around you that you can feel. Perhaps you feel sand giving way beneath your feet, or a cool breeze caressing your hair. Whatever you feel, try to identify four as specifically as possible. Really feel each one the best you can, and focus on every single detail. Notice how your hair tickles your face when the wind blows it, or how your entire body shifts as the sand does beneath you, compensating for the moving surface.

Hear

You should then focus on your hearing. Listen for three things around you and really take a few moments to hear them. You should pay attention to how they sound, following their melodies and rhythms the best you can. If you hear a bird trilling, focus on how its song rises and falls and how quickly it does.

Smell

Fourth, you will identify two different things around you that you can smell. Do you smell your perfume? What is the scent you have this time? Is it sweet? Musky, do you smell the scents of flowers warming in the sun? Try to identify as many elements of the scent as you can.

Feeling

Lastly, identify one thing within you that you are feeling at that moment. Are you angry? What is that anger doing to your body? Is it speeding your pulse up? Is it making you tense up? If you are sad, do you feel that hollow feeling spreading in your chest? Are your shoulders hunched? Figure out how you are feeling and how it affects your body.

With your mindfulness achieved, you will better be able to deal with whatever emotions your body was reacting to, choosing healthy, rational reactions as opposed to exploding or acting with emotional impulses.

Bettering Yourself

As you continue on your journey toward getting over the narcissist, you should put work into yourself. Attempting to better yourself gives you something else entirely to focus on, aside from the narcissist and will keep you busy. You will not have time to worry about the narcissist as much if you pick up a new hobby, such as learning to play the piano. You can even use this hobby to insert into time that you usually spent with the narcissist. For example, if you always spent Friday nights together eating takeout and watching your narcissist's favorite television program that you always secretly hated, you could instead use that weekly allotment of time to work on your new skill. Perhaps you choose this evening time to work on scales or try to learn the new songs your piano teacher has assigned for the week. Maybe instead, you look up video tutorials on how to play all sorts of songs that you listen to that remind you to stay strong.

Ultimately, learning a new skill and bettering yourself can only help you. You will never be worse off if you focus your energy and attention on learning a new skill, but if you use that time to focus on the past, dwell, and mope, you are likely to feel guilty about it later. Overall, it just makes more sense for you to spend that time focusing on things that will better you or can give you some new sense of self-worth to replace the damage the narcissist has done.

Affirmations

One last useful skill to learn when trying to get over the narcissist is learning how to form proper affirmations. An affirmation is a small sentence you use to remind yourself of an objective or goal or to reaffirm your own boundaries. They are usually quite short and are a common part of many different therapies, including cognitive-behavioral therapy, which teaches those who are using it to restructure their thinking. The idea here is to reverse the damage that the narcissist has done to you through all of his cruel words and demeaning comments. You listened to his cruelties for so long that you internalized them, and affirmations seek to do the exact opposite using the same concept. You will repeat your affirmations to yourself so often that you will convince yourself that they are true. Over time, you will begin to believe them, just like you believed the narcissist's disparaging comments. Affirmations have three key parts to them: They must be positive, self-directed, and present tense.

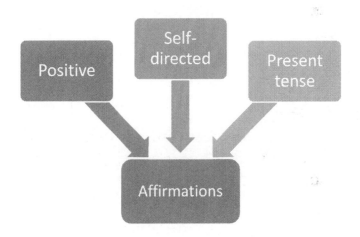

Positive

The reason you want to focus your affirmation on the positive is that it will shift your entire way of thinking. You will feel more positively if you think more positively. This uses the idea that you attract what you think. Think of it this way—in cognitive behavioral therapy; it is recognized that thoughts influence behaviors, which influence feelings, which influence thoughts, and the cycle continues. If you have a positive thought, it will lead to positive behavior, which will create a positive feeling, which will then create more positive thoughts. Positivity breed positivity, and ultimately, that can present itself all over your life. Your positivity will spread throughout your life, starting with that one simple positive affirmation, just as the narcissist's negativity spread through you.

Self-directed

Your affirmation must focus on yourself because ultimately, the only thing in this world you really have complete control over is yourself. When you are talking about yourself, you cannot come up with a way to deny its truth if you are thinking it. By focusing on yourself, you can make it come true. If you say that you will breathe before reacting to tense situations, you have the influence to make that happen. That is the important part here—you make it happen. If your affirmation focused on anyone else, you could not guarantee its validity, nor do you have any control over whether it happens. This makes it difficult to really trust or rely on.

Present tense

The reason for a present tense affirmation is that saying it at the moment prompts it to be true at that moment. If you say that you will do something, it is ambiguous whether that means immediately or sometime in the future. It is easier to sidestep that problem altogether and keep the affirmation present tense.

With these three rules in mind, you are ready to create your affirmations. You take all three aspects and stick them together to create a sentence like:

- *I deserve to be treated with respect, dignity, and kindness.*

- *I am enough the way that I am right now.*

- *The way I see the world is trustworthy, and I always trust my perceptions of what is happening around me.*

Each of these affirmations provides some sort of guidance and prompts you to believe in yourself more. You can create affirmations for virtually any situation that you think would benefit from them, and you should use them whenever you feel they would help. At the very least, make it a point to recite each affirmation to yourself at least ten times a day at the same time every day to make it a habit. For example, you could tell yourself, "I am enough the way that I am right now," every time you sit down in the car to drive to work. Every day, you repeat it several times to yourself, and eventually, that thought becomes just as reflexive and habitual as putting your seatbelt on when you get into your car. This is how you slowly shift your mind from the one poisoned by the narcissist into the healthier one you deserve.

Conclusion

Congratulations!! You have made it to the end of *Narcissistic Abuse Recovery!* Hopefully, the information you found within these pages has helped to open your eyes to the insidiousness of narcissistic abuse and all of the harm that it can inflict on those who suffer from it. If you are a victim, you may now be able to see the signs of abuse within yourself. If you are not a victim, perhaps you have realized that someone you know is. No matter what, you will be prepared to identify victims in the future, so you know that you can treat them with the compassion and kindness they will need to escape their own abusers.

Throughout this book, you were provided with a wide range of information. You learned some key parts of narcissistic personality disorder, as well as how to identify a narcissist in your midst. You learned how the narcissist abuses those around him, hoping to keep them within his grasp and under his spell at all times for his own selfish uses. You learned about how he sees people around him as little more than tools meant to be abused and discarded when they are no longer useful. Your eyes were opened to the possibility of physical abuse within a narcissistic relationship, as well as several of the different ways the narcissist's abuse can hurt another person.

Along with learning to spot the abuse, you were taught how to handle the abuse. You were given several skills to handle abuse at the moment as well as how to make yourself less desirable as an abuse victim to avoid the abuse altogether. There were several tools here for you, ranging from cutting off the narcissist to managing your expectations when an interaction is required for some reason.

You were also guided through how to recover from narcissistic abuse. You were taught about the stages of recovery, acknowledgment, determination, compassion, and modeling for others. You were given tips on how to heal from narcissistic abuse, ranging from self-care to finding support groups and practicing mindfulness. Lastly, you were taught how to move on from the narcissist and get on with your life.

All of the content in this book is intended to help you on your journey to healing. As you wrap up this book, do not forget to acknowledge your own worth. No matter how much the narcissist may tell you otherwise, you are worthy of love. You are worthy of happiness. You are worthy of respect. No matter how hard the narcissist tries to convince you otherwise, know that things can and will get better. You can see a world in which you are happy again. You can escape the narcissist's grasp and free yourself. It will take patience and perseverance, but you can free yourself from the narcissist's grasp if you are ready to take the leap. If you are ready, hold on to this book and everything you have learned within the pages, and jump into the unknown. It may be scary, but there is a whole world waiting for you once you escape from the narcissist's grasp. Good luck on your journey!

If you found this book useful or helpful in any way, a review is always appreciated!

Other publications by Debbie Brain:

- Narcissistic Abuse: The Survival Guide to Recognize Codependent Relationships, Disarming the Narcissists and Preventing Emotional and Psychological Abuses. No More Narcissism in Your Life!
- Narcissistic Relationship: Learn Fast to Rediscover Your True Self, Unlocking your Mental Barriers After Toxic Relationships. Let Another Mindset Enrich You Positively. There's Only One Life to Live!
- Dealing with a Narcissist: A Useful Guide to Discover Narcissism and Narcissistic Personality Disorder and Find Right Words that You Can Use to Change Affected Minds by High-Conflict Personalities

Manufactured by Amazon.ca
Bolton, ON